U.S Fish & Wildlife Service

Neonatal Mortality of Elk in Wyoming: Environmental, Population, and Predator Effects

Biological Technical Publication

BTP-R6007-2006

Bruce L. Smith[1, 7]

Elizabeth S. Williams[2, 8]

Katherine C. McFarland[3, 9]

Trent L. McDonald[4]

Guiming Wang[5, 10]

Tommy D. Moore[6, 11]

[1]   U.S. Fish and Wildlife Service, National Elk Refuge, Jackson, WY

[2]   Wyoming State Veterinary Laboratory, University of Wyoming, Laramie, WY

[3]   U.S. Fish and Wildlife Service, National Elk Refuge, Jackson, WY

[4]   Western Ecosystems Technology, Cheyenne, WY

[5]   Arkansas Tech University, Russellville, AR

[6]   Wyoming Game and Fish Department Laboratory, University of Wyoming, Laramie, WY

[7]   Current Address: Sheridan, MT 59749

[8]   Current Address: deceased

[9]   Current Address: National Park Service, Grand Teton National Park, Moose, WY

[10]   Current Address: Department of Wildlife and Fisheries, Mississippi State University, Mississippi State, MS

[11]   Current Address: Laramie, WY

Cover image: Elk calf
Photo credit: Bruce Smith/USFWS

Author Contact information:

Bruce L. Smith, (Current address) 44 Duncan District Road, Sheridan, MT 59749. Phone: (406) 842-5995, e-mail: elkmail@3rivers.net

Katherine C. McFarland, (Current address) National Park Service, Grand Teton National Park, Drawer 170, Moose, WY, 83012. Phone: (307) 733-3484, e-mail: katherine_mcfarland@nps.gov

Trent L. McDonald, Western Ecosystems Technology, 2003 Central Avenue, Cheyenne, WY 82001. Phone: (307) 755-9717, e-mail: tmcdonald@west-inc.com

Guiming Wang, Current Address: Thompson Hall, Room 273, Department of Wildlife and Fisheries, Mississippi State University, Mississippi State, MS 39762. Phone: (662) 325-0414, email: gwang@cfr.msstate.edu

Tommy D. Moore, PO Box 2421, Laramie, WY 82073. Phone: (307) 742-6057

Recommended citation:

Smith, B.L., E.S. Williams, K.C. McFarland, T.L. McDonald, G. Wang, and T.D. Moore. 2006. Neonatal mortality of elk in Wyoming: environmental, population, and predator effects. U.S. Department of Interior, U.S. Fish and Wildlife Service, Biological Technical Publication, BTP-R6007-2006, Washington, D.C.

For additional copies or information, contact:

Wayne J. King
USFWS Region 6
Regional Refuge Biologist
P.O. Box 25486
Denver Federal Center
Denver, Colorado 80225-0486
Phone: (303) 236-8102
Fax: (303) 236-4792
E-mail: wayne_j_king@fws.gov

Series Senior Technical Editor:

Stephanie L. Jones
USFWS, Region 6
Nongame Migratory Bird Coordinator
P.O. Box 25486
Denver Federal Center
Denver, Colorado 80225-0486

Table of Contents

Frequency of visitation (proportion of weeks visited during the sampling period) of black and grizzly bears at hair collection corrals in the East and West study areas during 1997 - 1999. We monitored all corrals weekly from approximately 1 June through 31 July 1998 and 1999 (8 weeks). In 1997, we monitored all hair collection corrals 1 June through the third week of July (7 weeks) except Granite Creek and Death Canyon, which we monitored only during July (4 weeks).

List of Figures

List of Tables

Executive Summary

Public concerns over large losses of wild ungulates to predators arise when restoring large carnivore species to former locations or population densities. During the 1990s, mountain lion (*Felis concolor*) and grizzly bear (*Ursus arctos*) numbers increased in Jackson Hole, Wyoming, and gray wolves (*Canis lupus*) were reintroduced to the Greater Yellowstone Ecosystem. We investigated effects of these predators, as well as black bears (*Ursus americanus*) and coyotes (*Canis latrans*), on mortality of an abundant and increasing prey species, elk (*Cervus elaphus*). We captured, radio-instrumented, and monitored survival of 145 elk neonates from 3 cohorts during 1990 - 1992, and 153 neonates from 3 cohorts during 1997 - 1999 when grizzly bears and lions were likely more common than during the earlier period of study. Neonatal (birth through 31 July) mortality of elk due to predation, disease, and accidents increased from 15.2 % to 27.5% ($P = 0.01$). Sixty-eight percent of all mortality during 1990 - 1992 resulted from predation by black bears and coyotes, compared to 76% during 1997-1999 by black bears, coyotes, grizzly bears, and mountain lions, a non-significant difference ($P = 0.49$). Weight gains of calves during the first week, but not birth weights, declined from 1990 - 1992 to 1997 - 1999. April temperatures were cooler, delaying spring green-up, and elk numbers were larger during 1997 - 1999 when weight gains and survival of calves declined. Calves that died were more likely to be male, below average birth weight, and had inferior serum nutritional indices. The change in neonatal calf survival reduced the annual growth rate of the Jackson elk herd from 1.26 to 1.23, yielding a decline in the annual increment of approximately 500 animals in a preparturition herd of 11,000 elk. Changes in mid-summer calf:100 cow ratios indicated a 39 - 45% greater decline in neonatal survival than measured among the radioed calves. We suggest increasing predation during the study was partially compensatory, given predator selection of inferior calves and increased mortality of cohorts with reduced first week growth rates. Reduced rate of first week weight gains of elk calves extended the duration of neonatal mortality by one month during 1997 - 1999, and may be as important in predisposing calves to predation and other mortality as low birth weights. Consequently, we conclude that increased predation was a proximate not an ultimate cause of declining neonatal survival during the 1990s. We recommend careful evaluation and hypothesis testing of predator effects on elk as restoration of large carnivores continues.

Acknowledgments

This work was generously supported by the Community Foundation of Jackson Hole, Grand Teton National Park, Rocky Mountain Elk Foundation, National Elk Refuge, University of Wyoming–National Park Service Research Center, Wildlife Forever, Wyoming Cooperative Fish and Wildlife Research Unit, Wyoming Game and Fish Department, National Rifle Association, Safari Club International, and the Wyoming State Veterinary Laboratory. Among those who provided field assistance, special thanks are due E. K. Bentley, A. N. Bethe, W. D. Helprin, D. D. Katnik, K. E. McGinley, A. E. Parker, S. M. Patla, A. M. Strassler, and S. G. Wolff. R. J. Hawkins of Hawkins and Powers Aviation safely and efficiently piloted our capture helicopter. G. L. Lust of Mountain Air Research piloted fixed-wing telemetry missions.

C. R. Anderson, R. G. Grogan, and L. S. Mills helped identify predator species from hair samples. J. G. Cook and T. J. Roffe provided insights into blood chemistry results. R. W. Klaver provided NDVI metrics. We thank S. H. Anderson, S. L. Cain, D. S. Moody, B. G. Reiswig, and T. L. Toman for administrative assistance. R. A. Garrott, B. K. Johnson, D. S. Moody, and T. K. Fuller provided helpful reviews and improvements of the manuscript. Finally, without the encouragement and support of R. J. Schiller, the second phase of this project may never have been initiated, much less completed. The use of trade names or commercial products in this publication are solely for the purpose of providing specific information and does not imply recommendation or endorsement by the U.S. Government.

Introduction

Large carnivores are considered keystone species that are vital to the integrity of many ecosystems (Estes 1996, Power et al. 1996). However, restoration and recovery of large North American carnivores has been met with skepticism and resistance by some Americans, particularly those that live closest to recovery areas and feel threatened by their presence (Bath 1991, Fisher 1995, U.S. Fish and Wildlife Service 1998). The most prevalent concerns are livestock depredations, financial loss to ranchers, human safety, and large losses of wild ungulate populations (Bath 1991, Braun 1991, Linnell et al. 1995, Pate et al. 1996, U.S. Fish and Wildlife Service 1998). Mech (1996) noted that the debate is not about whether predators affect their prey; they do. Rather, debate continues about the degree to which predation is compensatory, regulates prey populations in combination with other factors, and how predators may shape behavior and structure of prey populations.

Gaillard et al. (1998) in their review of population dynamics of large herbivores found that recruitment is the main target of limiting factors, both density-dependent and density-independent. Variation in recruitment is more often a consequence of changes in juvenile survival than fecundity (Sæther 1997). The rate of juvenile mortality often varies widely among populations of the same species (Geist 1971) which can significantly affect recruitment and the rate of increase of cervid populations (Caughley 1977). High neonatal losses can result from predation, adverse weather conditions, low birth weights and growth rates, altered immunocompetence of neonates, and inbreeding depression (Ralls et al. 1979, Clutton-Brock et al. 1992, Kunkel and Mech 1994, Sams et al. 1996, Sæther 1997, Singer et al. 1997, Gaillard et al. 1998). Large terrestrial predators, for example, appear capable of limiting prey populations to varying degrees (Gasaway 1992) and removal, addition, or changes in abundance of keystone predators can produce trophic cascades (Sinclair and Norton-Griffiths 1979, McNaughton 1985).

To elucidate predator effects on prey populations, Estes (1996) and Gaillard et al. (1998) advocated hypothesis testing in manipulative experiments that remove or add predators and compare results to unmanipulated controls. Yet scientists seldom have the opportunity to conduct such experiments with wild populations of large, valuable mammals. Documentation of predatory effects during fortuitous fluctuations in predator abundance, resulting from natural variation, over-exploitation or protection from exploitation by man, or reintroductions offer important opportunities for scientists to understand the role of predators in ecosystems (Estes 1996, Mech 1996). Such an opportunity presented itself to us with regard to predation on elk (*Cervus elaphus*).

In the Greater Yellowstone Ecosystem (GYE), grizzly bear (*Ursus arctos*) and mountain lion (*Felis concolor*) populations, following restriction of human exploitation, are recovering (Berger et al. 2001a, Clark et al. 1999, Murphy 1998, Schwartz et al. 2002), and gray wolves (*Canis lupus*) were successfully reintroduced in 1995 and 1996 (Bangs and Fritts 1996). Concerns about effects of predators on prey are nowhere more prevalent than in the GYE (Clark et al. 1999). The GYE supports eight species of wild ungulates, totaling some 164,000 animals, plus 230,000 cattle (*Bos taurus*) and 60,000 domestic sheep (*Ovis aires*) (Souvigney et al. 1997). Among the wild ungulates in the GYE, elk are most abundant, numbering 120,000 wintering animals in 25 herds (Toman et al. 1997). Among these, the Jackson herd is one of the largest elk herds in North America and one of the most widely known and studied (Boyce 1989, Lubow and Smith 2004).

Smith and Anderson (1996) documented cause-specific mortality of neonatal elk, including predation by black bears (*Ursus americanus*) and coyotes (*Canis latrans*), during an investigation of the Jackson elk herd in the early 1990s. The second phase of our study was prompted, in part, by a controversy surrounding grizzly bear depredation on two cattle grazing allotments in GTNP and adjacent Bridger-Teton National Forest south and east of Moran, Wyoming (Figure 1). Several hundred elk calved annually on those lands before cattle were turned out in late June and July. During the mid-1990s, grizzly bears began preying on bovine calves in these cattle grazing allotments (Anderson et al. 2002). We hypothesized that bears were attracted to the allotments to prey on elk calves then switched to bovines when most elk calves became difficult to capture.

Mountain lion numbers also appeared to increase during the 1990s in Jackson Hole (D. Brimeyer, pers. commun.). Because lions and grizzly bears are known to prey on elk neonates (Schlegel 1976, Singer et al. 1997), we endeavored to measure

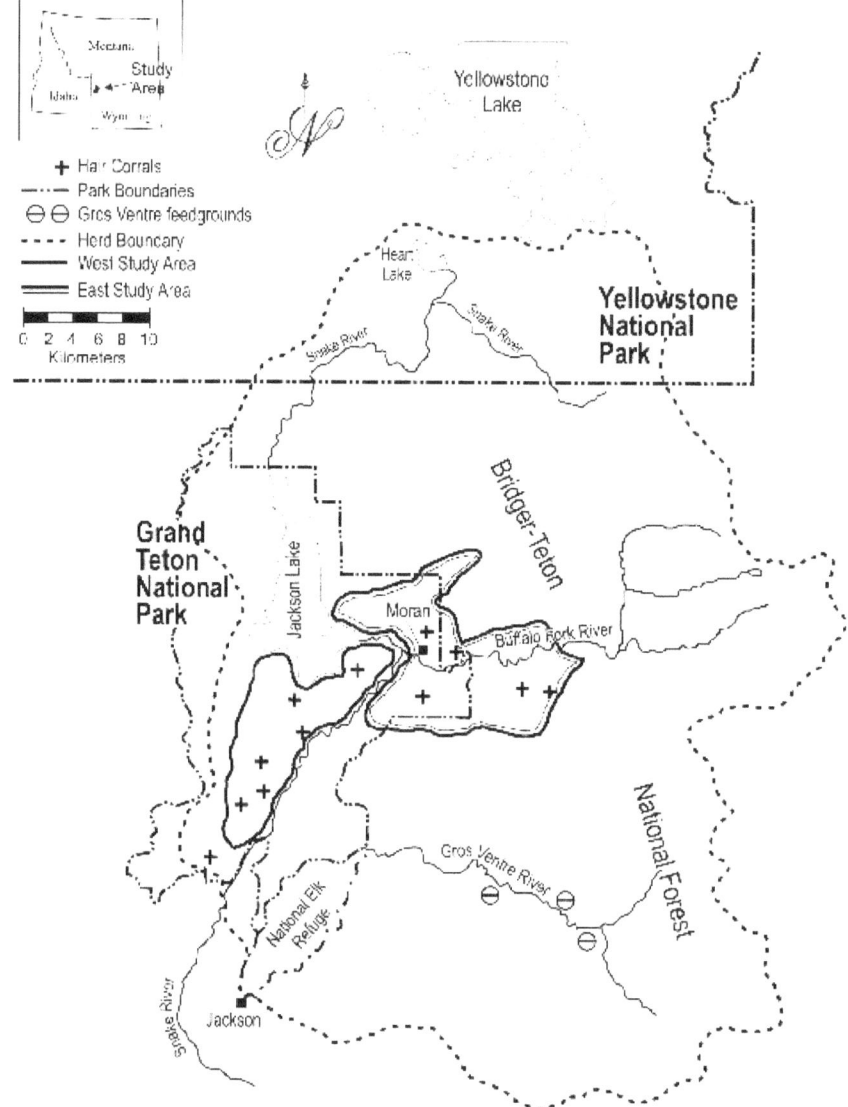

Figure 1. Area occupied by the Jackson elk herd showing hair collection corrals in the East and West study areas in which elk calves were captured during 1990 - 1992 and 1997 - 1999.

changes in neonatal mortality of the Jackson elk herd and measure allocation of this prey species among several species of carnivores.

Our objectives were to determine 1) the rate of predation by grizzly bears and mountain lions on elk calves, 2) whether such mortality was compensatory or additive to other sources of mortality, 3) any influence of environmental factors, calf physiological status, or population density on survival of elk neonates, and 4) if changes in neonatal mortality altered the surplus of elk from the Jackson herd available to hunters. We predicted the following:

1) Higher mortality would occur among elk neonates of lower birth weights and inferior nutritional status as indicated by blood serum chemistry.

2) Neonatal mortality would increase between study periods as predator populations increased.

3) Neonatal mortality would increase in our study area colonized by grizzly bears, compared to our grizzly-free study area, if grizzly bear predation is additive to other sources of mortality.

4) If predation represented additive mortality, it may be an important limiting influence on population growth and would reduce the harvestable surplus of elk available to hunters.

5) Calf mortality may show density dependence if it covaried with periods of different population sizes.

6) Calf mortality would vary in a density-independent way with cohort birth weight and with cohort weight gain, which covary with spring temperatures or foraging conditions.

7) Calf mortality would be partially or completely compensatory if spring weather conditions or inferior physiological condition predisposed calves to increased predation.

Study Area

Cole (1969), Boyce (1989), and Smith and Robbins (1994) described the boundaries, topography, climate, and vegetation communities of the Jackson elk herd unit, which encompasses 5,195 km^2 in the Snake River watershed of northwest Wyoming (Figure 1). Elk of the Jackson herd migrate 10 - 90 km between seasonal ranges (Smith and Anderson 2001). Between 13,000 and 16,200 elk were counted in the Jackson elk herd each winter during the 1990s, when population modeling indicated a herd size of 14,000 - 18,000 elk (Lubow and Smith 2004). About 70% of the herd is food supplemented in winter on the National Elk Refuge (NER) or on feedgrounds operated by the state of Wyoming in the Gros Ventre drainage. Elk typically arrive at feedgrounds during November and December and remain on and adjacent to feedgrounds through April or early May (Smith and Robbins 1994). They forage on new vegetative growth for several weeks following the termination of winter feeding about 1 April and then migrate to calving areas (Smith and Robbins 1994, Smith et al. 1997).

Our study was conducted in the Jackson Hole valley and foothills lying between the Teton Mountains on the west, the Gros Ventre Mountains and Mount Leidy Highlands on the east, and the Pinyon Peak Highlands on the north (Boyce 1989). Our two adjacent study areas, one east of the Snake River and Jackson Lake in both Grand Teton National Park (GTNP) and the Bridger-Teton National Forest (East SA), and one west of the Snake River in the Central Valley of GTNP (West SA, Figure 1), are important calving areas of the Jackson elk herd (Smith and Robbins 1994, Smith et al. 1997). Elevations range from 1950 to 2450 m. Vegetation communities include sagebrush (*Artemesia* spp.) grasslands, and aspen (*Populus tremuloides*) woodlands, interspersed with cottonwood (*Populus angustifolia*) and willow (*Salix* spp.) riparian zones, and coniferous forests of lodgepole pine (*Pinus contorta*), Douglas fir (*Pseudotsuga menziesii*), and Engelman spruce (*Picea engelmannii*). The climate is characterized by long cold winters and warm short summers. The reporting station in Moran, Wyoming (2069 m), is centrally located in the calving areas where we captured elk, and receives 617 mm of precipitation annually. January and July monthly temperatures at Moran average -10.2°C and 15.7°C, respectively (National Oceanic and Atmospheric Administration 1992).

Coyotes occupied both the East SA and West SA used by elk for calving (Smith and Anderson 1996).

During an investigation of coyote populations, Weaver (1977) found that coyotes were more abundant east of the Snake River than west of the River in 1973, but of similar abundance during the following two years, based on scat and scent station indices.

Black bears were common in both study areas (Smith and Anderson 1996). From genetic fingerprinting of hair collected at hair collection corrals in the East SA, a density of 6 - 10 black bears per 100 km^2 was estimated during the late 1990s (R. Grogan, pers. commun.). Density in the West SA was likely higher based on habitat differences and protection from hunting (S. L. Cain, pers. commun.).

An established mountain lion population inhabiting Jackson Hole probably increased during the course of our investigation. Hunters harvested three lions during 1972 - 1992 in Jackson Hole compared to 26 harvested, four natural mortalities, and four killed on highways during 1994 - 1999 (D. Brimeyer, pers. commun.). Mountain lion hunting seasons were similar during the 1990s (D. Brimeyer, pers. commun.). An ongoing ecological investigation of mountain lions in Jackson Hole indicated 4 - 5 resident adult lions inhabited the East SA, and another three lions likely inhabited the West SA (H. Quigley, pers. commun.).

Our study areas were located in the southern portion of the GYE. Grizzly bear numbers approximately doubled throughout the ecosystem during the 1990s (Table 1). Schwartz et al. (2002) noted that range expansion of grizzly bears was particularly evident during the 1990s in the southern portion of the ecosystem, including previously unoccupied areas of Wyoming. During the 1990s, grizzly bears began recolonizing former range and killing bovine calves in two cattle grazing allotments, the Elk Ranch East (in GTNP) and the Blackrock-Spread Creek (Bridger-Teton National Forest), which covered 450 km^2 south and east of Moran, Wyoming (Anderson et al. 2002). West SA (220 km^2) lay south and west of those allotments, whereas our East SA (260 km^2) was > 50% encompassed by those two grazing allotments (Figure 1). Anderson et al. (2002) reported that few sightings or grizzly bear conflicts and no documented livestock deaths associated with grizzly bears occurred from 1985 - 1991 in those grazing allotments. However, State of Wyoming personnel attributed deaths of six bovine calves and 26 additional cattle (25 calves, one cow) in 1993 to grizzly bear predation on those grazing allotments

Table 1. Numbers of female grizzly bears with cubs of the year and total estimated grizzly bear population in the Greater Yellowstone Ecosystem, 1989 - 1999.

Year	Females with cubs of the year[a]		Total number of cubs[a]	Estimated total population[b]
	Unduplicated no.	Total sightings		
1989	16	33	29	214
1990	25	53	58	238
1991	24	62	43	287
1992	25	39	60	377
1993	20	32	41	374
1994	20	34	47	341
1995	17	25	37	364
1996	33	56	72	425
1997	31	80	62	480
1998	35	86	70	427
1999	33	108	63	407

[a] Schwartz and Haroldson 2002
[b] U. S. Fish and Wildlife Service 2003

(Anderson et al. 2002). These depredations prompted a 3-year study of the situation by the Wyoming Game and Fish Department. During summers 1994 - 1996, 18 grizzly bears and 24 black bears were captured in snares and culvert traps on the allotments and 17 of each species were fitted with radio transmitters. Cattle losses continued and a grizzly bear documented killing cattle was captured and euthanized in GTNP in 1996 (Anderson et al. 2002).

Holm (1998) estimated that at least 15 grizzly bears and 21 - 25 black bears in 1995 and at least 16 grizzly bears and 19 - 21 black bears in 1996 used the two cattle allotments. Estimates of the number of grizzly bears frequenting East SA during 1997 - 1999 are unavailable and probably varied annually, based upon results of bear monitoring during 1994 - 1996 (Holm 1998, Anderson et al. 2002). Observations and radio telemetry locations of grizzly bears were uncommon in West SA during the 1990s (Schwartz et al. 2002, S. L. Cain, pers. commun.), allowing this area to serve as a comparative "grizzly-free" study site.

Gray wolves were reintroduced into Yellowstone National Park in 1995 and 1996. Wolves began dispersing into Jackson Hole in late 1998 (Smith et al. 1999). A pair of wolves, named the Teton Pack, denned near the center of East SA in early 1999 and whelped 5 pups. The adult male was killed in a vehicle collision in July 1999.

Grizzly bear in Yellowstone National Park. USFWS

Methods

Capture and Monitoring of Elk

During 1997 - 1999, we replicated the methodology and experimental design for capture and monitoring of elk used in a 1990 - 1992 investigation of cause-specific mortality of elk neonates (Smith and Anderson 1996). Each study used a Hiller 12-E helicopter to capture calves during late May and June of each year. During the 4 - 10 minutes we handled each calf, it was manually restrained, blindfolded, hobbled, sexed, and weighed to the nearest 0.25 kg. We aged calves according to Johnson (1951). We followed animal welfare protocol guidelines of the University of Wyoming and the U.S. Fish and Wildlife Service at the time of the study (Title 9 Code of Federal Regulations, Chapter 1, Subchapter A, Section 2.31).

Capture weights of 70 calves $\leq$ 1 day old were considered birth weights. We estimated birth weights of 248 calves > 1 day old by regressing capture weight on age (Smith et al. 1997). The regression slopes provided the sex-specific daily rates of gain of males and females.

Methods varied in two respects between the study periods. During 1990 - 1992, we instrumented each calf with an expandable radio collar (Telonics Inc.) weighing 230 g, 1.5% of an elk's birth weight (Smith et al. 1998). Batteries were configured and collars were designed to transmit pulse signals for $\geq$ 26 months. A mortality sensor with a 5-hour delay switch was integrated into each transmitter's circuitry. During 1997–1999, we fitted each calf with a 22-g ear tag transmitter (Advanced Telemetry Systems, Inc.). The transmitters remained silent while the calves were alive and active. When a transmitter remained immobile for > 4 hours, a mortality switch initiated transmission of a pulse signal. Garrott et al. (1985) found no difference in mortality rates and predation rates of mule deer (*Odocoileus hemionus*) fawns in Colorado, half of which were instrumented with radio collars and half instrumented with eartag transmitters. Survival was not affected by capture and radio-instrumenting of neonatal ungulates in previous studies (Ozoga and Clute 1988, Larsen and Gauthier 1989).

In addition, during 1997 - 1999, we drew 10 cc of blood from most calves by venipuncture of the jugular vein. We chilled and centrifuged the blood, then collected and froze the sera at –20° C. We submitted frozen sera to the Wyoming State Veterinary Laboratory within 1 month of collection for evaluation of physiological status and immunocompetence of calves. We used an automated analyzer for serum chemistry and electrolyte determinations (VetTest 8008 and VetLyte, Idexx). We analyzed levels of albumin, alkaline phophatase, aspartate aminotransferase, blood urea nitrogen, calcium, creatine kinase, gamma glutamylamin transferase (GGT), globulin, glucose, lactate dehydrogenase (LDH), magnesium, phosphorus, and total protein.

We employed null-peak telemetry systems at four fixed towers to monitor transmitter frequencies twice daily from capture of calves through 31 July, and once daily during August (Smith and Anderson 1996). We also monitored transmitter frequencies 2 - 3 times weekly from aircraft in areas beyond the reception range of telemetry towers.

Estimated Birth Weights and Rates of Gain

We estimated cohort daily rate of gain by regressing capture weights on capture age and using capture weights of calves $\leq$ 1 day old as birth weights (Smith et al. 1997). Slopes of regression lines were cohort daily rates of gain, which we compared for each sex between study periods using analysis of covariance. We estimated birth weight of each calf > 1 day old using the sex-specific daily rate of gain for the study period in which it was born. We used Student's *t* tests to compare mean monthly temperatures and precipitation during spring to identify factors influencing postpartum weight gain of calves during the two study periods.

In addition to measurements of monthly temperature and precipitation, we explored how climate and vegetation phenological changes potentially influenced weight gains and survival of calves by using satellite-derived normalized difference vegetation index (NDVI) data. The NDVI, derived from the National Oceanic and Atmospheric Administration's Advanced Very High Resolution Radiometer satellite sensor, have a 1 km x 1 km nominal spatial resolution and daily global coverage. NDVI metrics offer an efficient and objective means of evaluating phenological characteristics of vegetation on a broad scale (Reed et al. 1994). Due to the size of pixels, Advanced Very High Resolution Radiometer data are linked more to landscape processes than to individual plant communities (Malingreau and Belward 1992). Thus, we expected NDVI values to best correlate with our empirical forage measurements averaged over all plant communities sampled.

The NDVI has shown consistent correlation with vegetation biomass and dynamics in many ecosystems, and their response to climatic changes. The NDVI thus represents the first useful tool with which to couple climate, vegetation, and animal distribution and performances on broad spatial and temporal scales (Pettorelli et al. 2005). Metrics of interest to us were NDVI greeness values for the 8th (second and third weeks of April) and 9th (4th week of April and first week of May) composite periods of the year. We also calculated the rate of greenup as the straight line slope from 8th to the 12th (second and third weeks of June) composite period, based upon the NDVI values of each period. We assumed that each of these 3 metrics represented relative green forage quantity available each year (Reed et al. 1994).

Forensics

Upon detection of a mortality signal, we located and assessed the disposition of each calf as soon as possible ($\bar{x}$ =0.6 days in 1990, $\bar{x}$= 0.5 days in 1991, $\bar{x}$= 0.4 days in 1992, $\bar{x}$= 2.3 days in 1997, $\bar{x}$= 0.5 days in 1998, and $\bar{x}$= 1.0 days in 1999). At mortality sites, we conducted a thorough search for predator hair, feathers, tracks and scat, evidence of struggle and details of attack, and all remains of the carcass (Smith and Anderson 1996). We performed field necropsies on partially consumed carcasses, recording locations and measurements of canine punctures associated with attacks and noting feeding patterns. We collected and submitted tissue samples, and froze and sent intact carcasses to the Wyoming State Veterinary Lab for necropsy and diagnostic tests. We identified hair samples to species under a microscope, based on color, texture, and scale patterns of the medulla and cuticle (Moore et al. 1974). To identify species of ambiguous hair samples, we subjected them to microsatellite analysis of mitochondrial DNA at the University of Montana's Carnivore Conservation Genetics Laboratory (Mills et al. 2000).

Bear Distribution

To document presence of grizzly bears in both the West SA and East SA, we constructed 12 hair collection corrals (HCCs) (Woods et al. 1999) (Figure 1). Seven were located in the West SA and five in the East SA. A 3.8-l plastic milk jug, nearly filled with bovine blood, was suspended by rope between two trees over the center of each HCC and beyond the reach of a tall bear (Wyoming Game and Fish Department 1996). We replaced jugs of bovine blood with fresh blood every three weeks.

We visited HCCs weekly from approximately 1 June through 31 July 1997 - 1999. We removed, individually bagged, and submitted hair samples captured by the barbed wire for microscopic identification of species as described above.

Survival and Mortality Analyses

We monitored calf survival from birth through 31 August each year but report neonatal survival from birth through 31 July, after which date mortality

ceased. Variables measured during both studies that may affect survival included sex of the animal, birth weight, period of study (1990 - 1992 or 1997 - 1999), study area where the elk was captured (East SA or West SA), and birth period. Birth period categorized the birth date of each elk among the first, middle, or last third of all captures. Because the temporal distribution of captures varied annually with parturition chronology and flying conditions (27 May - 25 June 1990, 26 May - 9 June 1991, 27 May - 6 June 1992, 28 May - 7 June 1997, 26 May - 6 June 1998, and 26 May - 13 June 1999), we adjusted the dates encompassed by the first, middle, and last third of the calving season somewhat annually to equalize sample sizes by birth period.

We investigated factors influencing the survival of elk during their first summer of life using a Cox proportional hazards (PH) model (Cox and Oakes 1984, Collett 1994). Birth was time zero, t_0, in the PH model. Assuming $h_i(t)$ is the instantaneous probability of death for individual i at time t (called the hazard function), and that the i-th individual is associated with a measured covariate vector $x_I = (x_{i1}, x_{i2}, ..., x_{ip})$, the Cox PH model is

$$h_i(t) = h_0(t)\ exp(\beta_1 x_{i1} + \beta_2 x_{i2} + ... + \beta_p x_{ip})$$

where $h_0(t)$ is called the baseline hazard and corresponds to the hazard function of an individual with covariate vector $x_I = (0, 0, ..., 0)$.

The Cox PH model has been called semi-parametric because the distribution of lifetimes and the baseline hazard function are unspecified. The PH model derives its name from the fact that if $h_i(t)$ and $h_j(t)$ differ only because $x_{il} = x_{jl} + 1$, the hazard ratio, $h_i(t)/ h_j(t) = exp(\beta_l)$, does not depend upon time. Hence, $h_i(t)$ and $h_j(t)$ are proportional through time and differ only by a multiplicative constant. This proportionality of hazard functions is a basic assumption of the Cox PH model, the violation of which can lead to errant results. The proportional hazards assumption was assessed by plotting scaled Schoenfeld residuals versus survival times, and computing a chi-square significance test for the resulting correlation (Grambsch and Therneau 1994)

If the proportional hazards assumption of the Cox PH model was not satisfied, a stratified Cox PH model was estimated that assumed a different baseline hazard function for individuals in different strata. Under the stratified Cox PH model, proportionality of hazard functions was assumed among individuals in the same stratum. A drawback of the stratified Cox PH model was that the relationship between hazard and the variable used to define the strata could not be estimated directly. In this case, Kaplan-Meier curves (Cox and Oakes 1984, Collett 1994) were computed for each stratum and the difference in survival among strata was tested using the log-rank test (Collett 1994).

Hypotheses of the form H_0: $\beta_l = 0$ were tested using likelihood ratio tests (Collett 1994). We computed likelihood ratio tests as $-2ln(L_1) + 2ln(L_2)$, where

L_1 represents the statistical likelihood of a Cox PH model that does not contain β_1 and L_2 represents the statistical likelihood of a Cox PH model that does contain β_1. We then compared the resulting value to a chi-square distribution. We computed tests of factors involving more than two levels (and hence more than one β_1) using L_1 and L_2 that differed by two or more coefficients. All two-way interactions of variables were initially considered in the Cox PH model. We removed any variables that were not significant in the Cox PH model one-at-a-time in a backward step-wise fashion to arrive at a final Cox PH model.

We classified each mortality as either predation mortality or not. For this analysis, we retained non-predation mortalities in the analysis because like animals that survived the entire neonatal period (until 31 July each year), they did not succumb to predation. We censored the non-predation mortalities at the date of death. We investigated the instantaneous probability of death by predation using a Cox PH model applied to predation mortalities. Due to the small number of predation mortalities, we categorized birth weight as either < 16.0 kg (the average birth weight), or ≥ 16.0 kg. We checked the proportional hazards assumption at each stage of the analysis. We eliminated terms in the Cox PH model that were non-significant.

Population Size and Recruitment
Each February, observers riding on feeding vehicles systematically counted the number of elk wintering on the NER and on three feeding grounds in the Gros Ventre drainage and classified them as calves, females (≥ 1 year old), yearling males, and mature males (Figure 1; Boyce 1989, Smith and McDonald 2002). Elk wintering at other locations were surveyed and classified from a Bell B1 helicopter (Wyoming Game and Fish Department 2000, Lubow and Smith 2004). We used the Wyoming Game and Fish Department (2000) survey results and other data to model the winter population size with POP II software program (Bartholow 1997). We tested for difference in the mean number of elk in the Jackson herd during the 5-year interval (1985-1989 and 1992-1996) preceding each of our two study periods (1990 - 1992 and 1997 - 1999) to assess lag effects in population influences on recruitment. We chose a 5-year interval because ungulate species can experience time lags of 3 - 10 years in density-dependent population responses (Saether 1997).

We annually counted and classified elk that summered in our study areas in GTNP during the first week of August 1991 - 1999 from a Bell Jet Ranger helicopter (Smith and Anderson 1996). Recruitment rates during winter and summer are expressed as number of calves:100 females ≥ 1 year old. We compared calf:100 cow ratios in August to expected reproduction from pregnancy rates (Smith and Robbins 1994). This provided a second measure of calf survival from birth through July that we compared to survival of radioed calves.

We assessed pregnancy rate of 159 ≥ 2-year-old elk captured in a corral trap on the NER during

February 1998 - 2002 from serum assays of pregnancy-specific protein-B (Noyes et al. 1997). We compared results to pregnancy estimates of a group of 318 ≥ 2-year-old elk captured on NER during 1978 - 1982 (Smith and Robbins 1994). This comparison served to evaluate if fecundity of females had changed over time, which could influence recruitment and our population modeling efforts. We also compared pregnancy status of 52 yearling females during 1978 - 1982 to 42 yearlings captured and tested during 1998 - 2002.

Population Modeling
We built an individual based model to project the effects of increased neonatal mortality on the population growth rate of the Jackson elk herd. From the average of winter population classification counts obtained during the 1990s, we partitioned the elk population into six age-sex classes: male and female calves (each sex constituting 7.5% of the herd), yearling males (males > 1 but < 2 years old, 5.6%), yearling females (5.6%), bulls (14.5%), and cows (59.3%). We assumed a 1:1 sex ratio at birth (Smith et al. 1996). We estimated 1% prehunting season mortality (1 August - 10 September) for each age-sex class (Smith and Robbins 1994, Smith and Anderson 1998). We estimated a herd pregnancy rate of 63% (17% for yearlings and 87% for 2+ year-old elk, reduced by 7% to account for brucellosis-caused fetal losses, Oldemeyer et al. 1993, Smith and Robbins 1994). To isolate the influence of change in neonatal survival on population growth, we held constant over the two study periods all population parameters except neonatal survival. We considered how change in neonatal survival from the early 1990s to the late 1990s would alter the annual harvestable surplus of a preparturition population size of 11,000 elk. We used 11,000 elk as that is the population objective established by the Wyoming Game and Fish Commission for the Jackson herd (Wyoming Game and Fish Department 2000).

Harvestable Surplus— We sought to estimate how a change in neonatal survival between study periods would change the number of elk available to hunters. To do so, we used Monte Carlo simulations to estimate the number of elk surviving and reproducing during the time period 20 May (onset of parturition) to 10 September (start of hunting season). The number of surviving elk represented the population size on 10 September. In the simulations, we generated random numbers and compared them with survival rates of each age-sex group, as reported by Smith and Anderson (1998) for radioed elk older than calves, to determine fate (death or survival) of each individual in the group. The fate of newborn calves was decided by comparing the random numbers with measured mortality of radioed calves from birth to 10 September. We used the observed sex-specific neonatal mortality during each study period in the simulations. We determined reproductive status of each yearling and adult female from a separate set of random numbers.

From 1,000 Monte Carlo simulations, we generated estimates of mean herd size in September and mean population growth rate for a pre-parturition herd size of 11,000 elk for 1990 - 1992 and for 1997 - 1999. We computed the finite rate of increase of the elk population from May to September for each iteration of the simulations, from the equation

$$r = (N_{t+1} - N_t)/N_t$$

The increase in the population size from 19 May to 10 September was considered equivalent to the harvestable surplus.

Annual Population Growth—We constructed Lefkovitch transmission matrices (Lefkovitch 1965) of survival of 3 age classes of female elk for the early 1990s and the late 1990s. Annual survival rates of yearling and adult females reported by Smith and Anderson (1998) during 1990 - 1992 were used for both study periods. Likewise, Smith and Anderson (1998) reported annual survival of calves during 1990 - 1992 as the sum of neonatal, fall, and winter survival. For 1997 - 1999, we used the same estimates of calf fall and winter survival. Annual survival of female calves (s_1) in the late 1990s was thus determined as the product of the seasonal survival rates

$$s_1 = s_{neo}\, s_f\, s_w$$

where s_{neo} = neonatal survival, s_f = survival during the fall, and s_w = over-winter survival. We derived rates of neonatal survival (s_{neo}) for each study period from radioed animals as measured in the present investigation. Fall (s_f) and winter (s_w) survival of calves reported by Smith and Anderson (1998) during 1990 - 1992 were applied to both study periods. Consequently, only neonatal survival was permitted to differ between 1990 - 1992 and 1997 - 1999.

The Lefkovitch matrix for 1990 - 1992 is

$$\begin{bmatrix} 0 & f_2 & f_3 \\ s_1 & 0 & 0 \\ 0 & s_2 & s_3 \end{bmatrix} = \begin{bmatrix} 0 & 0.17 & 0.81 \\ 0.66 & 0 & 0 \\ 0 & 0.89 & 0.94 \end{bmatrix}$$

The Lefkovitch matrix for 1997 - 1999 is

$$\begin{bmatrix} 0 & f_2 & f_3 \\ s_1 & 0 & 0 \\ 0 & s_2 & s_3 \end{bmatrix} = \begin{bmatrix} 0 & 0.17 & 0.81 \\ 0.56 & 0 & 0 \\ 0 & 0.89 & 0.94 \end{bmatrix}$$

where f_2 and f_3 are the fecundity of yearling and adult females, respectively; s_1, s_2, and s_3 are the survival rates of calves, yearlings and adults, respectively. The dominant eigenvalues of the above Lefkovitch matrices were the annual finite rates of increase (λ) of the elk populations (Caswell 2001).

We conducted sensitivity analyses to determine how sensitive the finite rates of increase of the elk population were to the change in each nonzero element (or vital rate of elk) in the transmission matrices. The sensitivity of λ to a vital rate is determined by (Caswell 2001)

$$\frac{\partial \lambda}{\partial a_{ij}} = \frac{v_i w_j}{\langle \mathbf{w}, \mathbf{v} \rangle}$$

Where $\frac{\partial \lambda}{\partial a_{ij}}$ is the sensitivity of the finite rate of increase to changes in element a_{ij} of the Lefkovitch matrix; v_i is the ith element of the left eigenvector of the Lefkovitch matrix; w_j the jth element of the right eigenvector of the Lefkovitch matrix; and $\langle \mathbf{w}, \mathbf{v} \rangle$ is the scalar product of the right and left eigenvectors (Caswell 2001). The larger the sensitivity index $\frac{\partial \lambda}{\partial a_{ij}}$ the more sensitive λ was to the vital rate.

Acquiring large, unbiased samples of newborn ungulates in wildland settings to assess survival and correlates with survival is difficult. We chose $P < 0.10$ as significant for statistical tests rather than a smaller P value, due to the biological and management importance of any such findings regarding survival rates. We used $P < 0.05$ when addressing differences in physical traits of calves between study periods and between the sexes.

Results

Birth Weights

We captured and radio-tagged 318 neonatal elk (Table 2). We censored from survival analyses 19 of 164 calves captured (53 in 1990, 62 in 1991, and 49 in 1992) during the early 1990s that cast their radios prior to 31 July of their birth year. We also censored 1 of 154 elk captured (46 in 1997, 51 in 1998, and 57 in 1999) during the late 1990s. Calves captured during 1990-1992 were similar in age ($\bar{x}$= 3.3 days $\pm$ 0.16 SE; t = 1.77, 317 df, P = 0.08) to those captured during 1997-1999 ($\bar{x}$= 3.0 $\pm$ 0.15 SE).

Capture weights of males (t = 1.96, 163 df, P = 0.048) and females (t = 3.29, 152 df, P = 0.001) were heavier during 1990 - 1992 than during 1997 - 1999. However, capture weights of calves $\leq$ 1-day-old (considered birth weights) were similar during the early 1990s (22 males, 11 females) and late 1990s (16 males, 21 females) (males: t = 0.09, P = 0.93;

females: t = 1.3, P = 0.2). When capture weights of calves > 1-day-old were age-corrected, using daily rates of gain calculated for each study period, estimated birth weights were no different between the two time periods for males (t = 0.29, 163 df, P = 0.77 and females (t = 1.29, 152 df, P = 0.2; Table 2). Within study periods, estimated birth weights differed by sex (Table 2). Estimated birth weights for males (P > 0.6) and females (P > 0.8) were similar in the East and West study areas during 1990 - 1992 and during 1997 - 1999 (Table 2).

Growth and Physiological Status of Calves

Mean daily rate of gain increased linearly in all 6 years (P < 0.001), but was more variable during 1997 - 1999 (male: r^2 = 0.25–0.50; female: r^2 = 0.28–0.49) compared to 1990 - 1992 (male: r^2 = 0.59–0.63; female: r^2 = 0.41–0.59). Mean daily rate of gain of males exceeded that of females during the early

Table 2. Estimated birth weights and daily rates of gain (kg/day) of newborn elk calves captured in the Jackson elk herd, northwest Wyoming. All captured neonates are represented, including those that later cast their radio transmitters. Birth weights were no different (P = 0.16 - 0.8) for either sex between study periods or between study areas.

Study period	Study area	Sex	n	Birth weight (kg) $\bar{x}$	Birth weight (kg) SE	Rate of gain $\bar{x}$	Rate of gain SE
1990 - 1992	Both	Male	88	16.8 [a]	0.27	1.64 [c]	0.14
1997 - 1999	Both	Male	76	16.6 [b]	0.29	1.18 [c]	0.18
1990 - 1992	Both	Female	76	15.8 [a]	0.28	1.31 [d]	0.14
1997 - 1999	Both	Female	78	15.2 [b]	0.31	1.09 [d]	0.18
1990 - 1992	Both	Both	164	16.3	0.19	1.39 [e]	0.11
1997 - 1999	Both	Both	154	15.9	0.22	1.17 [e]	0.13
1990 - 1992	East	Male	44	16.7	0.38		
1990 - 1992	West	Male	45	16.8	0.39		
1990 - 1992	East	Female	23	15.9	0.44		
1990 - 1992	West	Female	53	15.7	0.32		
1997 - 1999	East	Male	37	16.5	0.43		
1997 - 1999	West	Male	39	16.8	0.40		
1997 - 1999	East	Female	27	15.3	0.56		
1997 - 1999	West	Female	51	15.2	0.37		

[a] Birth weights of males and females were different (t = 2.72, 163 df, P = 0.007)
[b] Birth weights of males and females were different (t = 3.32, 152 df, P = 0.001)
[c] Rates of gain for males were different ($F_{1,87}$ = 10.09, P = 0.002) between study periods.
[d] Rates of gain for females were not different ($F_{1,76}$ = 1.44, P = 0.23).
[e] Rates of gain for all calves were different ($F_{1,163}$ = 3.93, P = 0.049).

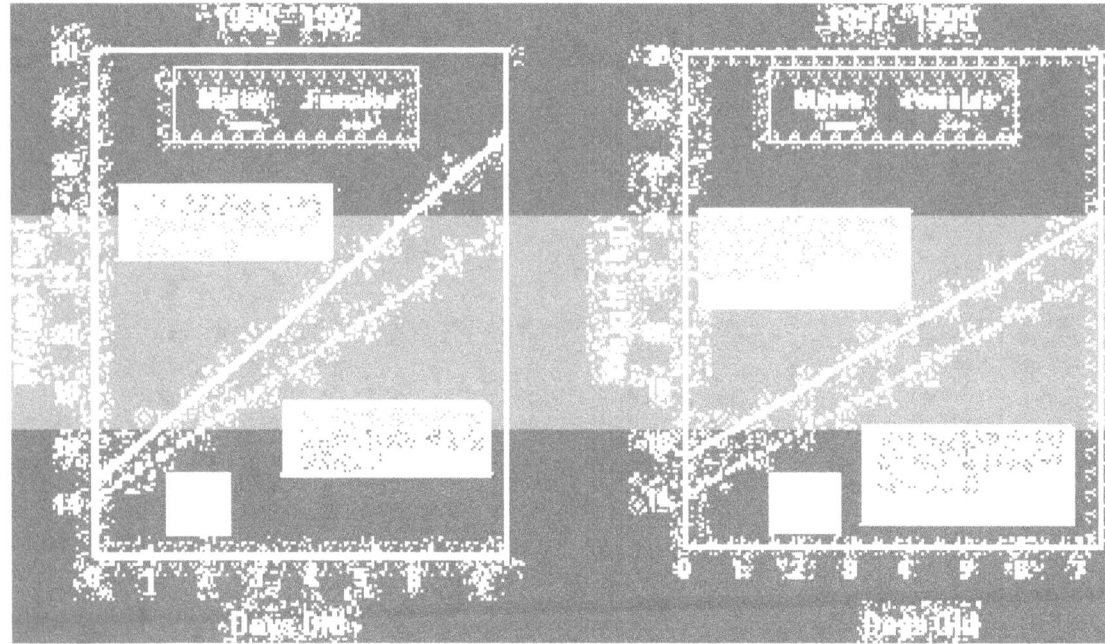

Figure 2. Weights of elk calves captured during 1990 - 1992 and 1997 - 1999 regressed on age of the calves at birth. Weights of calves ≤ 1 day old were considered birth weights. Slopes of the equations are estimated cohort daily rates of gain for males and females during the first week of life.

1990s ($F_{1,74}$ = 4.45, P = 0.037), but not during the late 1990s ($F_{1,76}$ = 0.11, P = 0.7; Figure 2). Estimated daily rates of gain during the late 1990s declined from the early 1990s in both sexes, significantly so for males and sexes combined (Table 2).

We drew blood for serum assays from 84 of 154 calves (67 that survived and 17 that died) captured during 1997 – 1999. Analyses of passive transfer of immunoglobulins showed no significant differences in gamma-globulin (t = 1.6, P = 0.12) or gamma-glutamyl transferase (t = 1.7, P = 0.1) concentrations between 67 neonates that survived and 17 that died. There were also no differences in these immunological attributes between study areas or sex (P > 0.7 for all tests). We also assessed exposure to leptospirosis and bovine viral diarrhea I and bovine viral diarrhea II and found no differences between calves that survived and those that died, between sexes, and between study areas (P = 0.22 – 0.6 for all tests). However, surviving calves had higher total serum protein, phosphorus, alkaline phosphatase, and glucose and lower levels of blood urea nitrogen and lactate dehydrogenase compared to mortalities (Table 3). Serum attributes were not related to estimated calf birth weights.

Predator Abundance
We collected 537 hair samples from black bears and 8 hair samples from grizzly bears at 12 HCCs. Based on HCC visitations, black bears were twice as abundant in the West SA as the East SA during 1997 – 1999 (Appendix A). Frequency of grizzly bear visitation at HCCs averaged 0.02 compared to 0.18 and 0.37 for black bears in the East and West SA, respectively (Appendix A).

Mortality Factors
Twenty-two of 145 (15.2%) elk captured and radio-instrumented during 1990 - 1992 died between birth and 31 July of their birth year compared to 42 of 153 (27.5%; X^2 = 0.6.7, P = 0.01) that died during 1997 - 1999 (Table 4, Appendix B). Likewise the number of predator-caused deaths increased from 1990 - 1992 [15 of 145 (10.3%)] to 1997 - 1999 [32 of 153 (20.9%); X^2 = 0.6.3, P = 0.012]. However, the proportion of all mortalities per study period due to predation was similar between periods (68% vs. 76%, X^2 = 0.48, P = 0.49), whereas the proportion of deaths from disease declined (27% vs. 14%, Fisher's exact test P = 0.034) (Figure 3, Appendix B). Bears of both species were responsible for 11 of 15 (73%) and 23 of 32 (72%) predator kills during 1990 - 1992 and 1997 - 1999, respectively. The proportion of marked calves killed by bears increased (Fisher's exact test P = 0.038) from 1990 - 1992 to 1997 - 1999 in the grizzly bear occupied East SA, but not in the West SA (P = 0.61; Table 5).

Grizzly bears killed 6 radioed calves (all during 1997 - 1999), 5 in the East SA and 1 calf just west of the Snake River that separated the West and East study areas (Table 5, Appendix C). However, the proportion of calves killed by both species of bears did not differ between study areas during 1997 - 1999 (Fisher's exact test P = 0.17), nor did mortality from all causes differ (Fisher's exact test P = 0.22, Figure 3).

We considered sex, birth period, estimated birth weight, study period, and study area as variables that may have contributed to mortality. No two-way interactions of these variables were significant in the Cox PH model. Among main effects, neither study area (P = 0.81) nor birth period (P = 0.28)

Table 3. Serum chemistries of 84 elk calves captured during 1997 - 1999 in the Jackson elk herd, northwest Wyoming. We used Student's *t* tests to compare means of calves that survived (*n* = 67) and those that died (*n* = 17) during the neonatal period (birth to 31 July) and present results of each test producing a *P* value < 0.10.

Serum attribute	Calves that survived		Calves that died		
	$\bar{x}$	SD	$\bar{x}$	SD	*P* value
Alkaline phosphatase (U/L)	903	531	654	336	0.022
Lactate dehydrogenase (U/L)	1168	350	1784	1149	0.052
Glucose (mg/dl)	148.8	27.0	130.4	40.5	0.092
Blood urea nitrogen (mg/dL)	16.4	5.8	24.3	16.3	0.063
Total protein (g/dL)	6.46	0.89	5.95	0.95	0.057
Phosphorus (mg/dL)	9.54	1.41	8.37	1.52	0.009

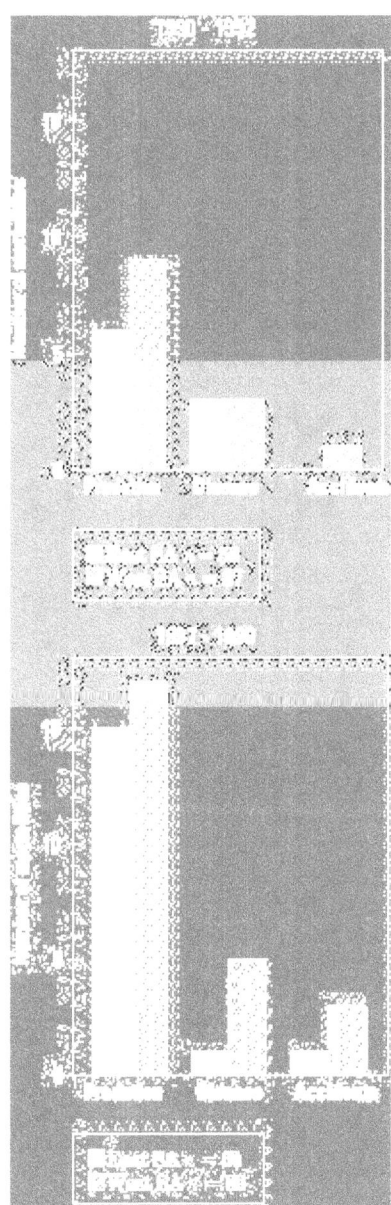

Figure 3. Neonatal mortality (birth through 31 July of the birth year) of radioed elk calves captured in the East (East SA) and West (West SA) study areas during 1990 - 1992 and 1997 - 1999.

contributed significantly to mortality. Of the remaining 3 variables, we could not reject the assumption of proportional hazards for sex (*P* = 0.33) and birth weight (*P* = 0.45), but we did reject proportional hazards for study period (*P* = 0.03). The test of the proportional hazards assumption implied that the elk survival curve's shape changed significantly between 1990 - 1992 and 1997 - 1999. A log-rank test of the Kaplan-Meier survival curves confirmed that survival of elk declined from 1990 - 1992 to 1997 - 1999 (*P* = 0.01). A plot of the estimated Kaplan-Meier curves for each study period revealed that survival of calves during 1990 - 1992 "flattened" at approximately 30 days, while survival of calves during 1997 - 1999 continued to fall until approximately 60 days postpartum (Figure 4).

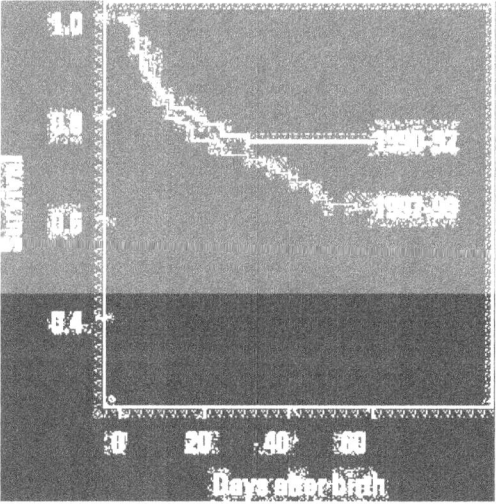

Figure 4. Survival of elk (sexes combined) from birth to approximately 60 days of age during 1990 - 1992 and 1997 - 1999. Log-rank test of difference was significant (*P* = 0.01).

We fit a stratified Cox PH model that satisfied the proportionality assumption within strata, with study period defining the strata. In the stratified model, both sex (*P* = 0.02) and birth weight (*P* = 0.001) were significant factors. When we combined the early 1990s and late 1990s study periods, the instantaneous probability of survival was estimated

Table 4. Sex-specific neonatal mortality of radioed elk from the Jackson elk herd, northwest Wyoming, during 1990 - 1992 and 1997 - 1999. Chi-square tests were used to compare the proportion of calves of each sex that died between study periods.

	Number of males		Number of females	
Year	Marked	Died (%)	Marked	Died (%)
1990	26	2	24	3
1991	29	9	25	3
1992	22	5	19	0
1997	23	9	23	6
1998	24	5	27	7
1999	29	8	27	7
1990 - 1992	77	16 (20.8)[a]	68	6 (8.8)[b]
1997 - 1999	76	22 (28.9)[a]	77	20 (26.0)[b]

[a] $X^2 = 1.4$, Fisher's exact test $P = 0.27$
[b] $X^2 = 7.2$, Fisher's exact test $P = 0.009$

Table 5. Predation on neonatal elk (sexes combined) by black bears and by black and grizzly bears combined during 1990 - 1992 and 1997 - 1999 in the East and West Study Areas of the Jackson elk herd, northwest Wyoming.

	1990 - 1992		1997 - 1999		All years		1990-1992	1997-1999
Variable	East	West	East	West	East	West	Both	Both
No. captured	67	97	64	90	131	187	164	154
No. cast radios	9	10		1	9	11	19	1
Black bear kills	4	7	7	9	11	16	11	16
% black bear predation	6.9	8.0	10.9	10.1	9.0	9.1	7.6	10.4
Black and grizzly bear kills	4	7	13[a]	10	17	17	11	23
% black and grizzly predation	6.9	8.0	20.3	11.2	13.9	9.7	7.6	15.0

[a] Includes one predation by a bear of undetermined species.

to be 83% (approximate 95% CI = 9.6% to 205%) greater for females than it was for males. The instantaneous probability of survival increased by 15.4% (approximate 95% CI = 7.2% to 22.8%) for every additional kilogram of weight at birth (Figure 5). The effect of birth weight on survival was greater at lower birth weights (Figure 6, Table 6). Contrary to no difference in the early 1990s ($P = 0.11$ and 0.42), capture weights ($t = 3.0$, 151 df, $P = 0.003$) and estimated birth weights ($t = 3.5$, 151 df, $P = 0.001$) of surviving calves were greater than weights of dying calves during the late 1990s by 1.8 kg and 1.7 kg, respectively. Elk that died from predation (14.6 kg $\pm$ 0.5 SE), disease (14.7 kg $\pm$ 1.0 SE), and accidents (14.7 kg $\pm$ 1.3 SE) were of similar birth weights ($F_{2,60} = 0.003$, $P = 0.99$).

The instantaneous probability of death by predation was greater in the later study period ($P = 0.012$, log-rank test), but was not related to sex of the animal ($P = 0.12$). The probability of death by predation during 1990 - 1992 peaked at 9.5% for elk calves that were approximately 15 days old (Figure 7). The probability of death by predation during 1997 - 1999 peaked at 21.2% for elk calves that were approximately 55 days old (Figure 7). Predation by black bears and by black and grizzly bears combined increased during the 1990s (Table 5).

Weather Effects on Survival
Although birth weights were the same, daily cohort rate of weight gain (sexes combined) declined from the early 1990s to the late 1990s ($r^2 = 0.49$, $F_{1,163} = 3.93$, $P = 0.049$; Table 2). Lower weight gains of calves during the late 1990s coincided with cooler April temperatures ($t = 2.8$, 4 df, $P = 0.05$) and with higher elk numbers in the Jackson herd during the 5 years preceding each study period ($t = 2.57$, 8 df, $P = 0.033$, Table 7). Neither the daily ration ($t = 0.59$, 4 df, $P = 0.59$) nor number of days elk were fed at the NER ($t = 0.07$, 4 df, $P = 0.95$) differed between the early 1990s and late 1990s study periods (Table 7). The proportion of female calves that died increased from the early 1990s to the late 1990s

$(X^2 = 7.2$, df $= 1$, $P < 0.01$, Table 4). Annual survival of female calves positively correlated with their mean cohort weight gains ($r^2 = 0.71$, $F_{1,4} = 9.9$, $P = 0.035$). Annual survival of all calves positively correlated with mean monthly April temperature ($r^2 = 0.89$, $F_{1,4} = 34.0$, $P < 0.01$; Figure 8). Annual predation by black bears ($F_{1,4} = 11.1$, $P = 0.029$) and by both species of bears ($F_{1,4} = 651.7$, $P < 0.002$) varied inversely with mean monthly April temperature (Figure 9), and with NDVI during the second and third weeks of April ($F_{1,4} = 42.6$, $P < 0.003$ and $F_{1,4} = 23.7$, $P < 0.008$, respectively, Figure 9). April is the month during which ambient temperatures are generally sufficient to produce abundant spring green-up in Jackson Hole (Figure 8). Other NDVI metrics did not produce significant relationships to elk survival.

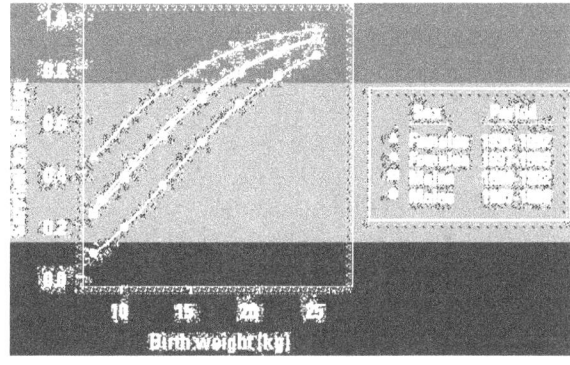

Figure 5. Relationship of birth weight of male and female calves of the Jackson elk herd to probability of survival from birth to 31 July of their birth year during 1990 - 1992 and 1997 - 1999. We estimated survival curves from the stratified Cox proportional hazards model.

Table 6. Estimated survival probabilities (95% confidence intervals) from birth to 60 days of age for radioed elk calves of different birth weights during 1990 - 1992 and 1997 - 1999. We computed estimates from the stratified Cox proportional hazards model.

Sex	Birth weight (kg)	1990 - 1992		1997 - 1999	
		n	Survival	n	Survival
Female	>8 to 12	4	0.57 (0.38 - 0.86)	11	0.39 (0.22 - 0.67)
Female	>12 to 16	36	0.75 (0.65 - 0.87)	41	0.61 (0.51 - 0.74)
Female	>16 to 20	35	0.86 (0.80 - 0.93)	22	0.78 (0.69 - 0.88)
Female	>20 to 24	1	0.93 (0.88 - 0.98)	3	0.88 (0.80 - 0.97)
Male	>8 to 12	3	0.36 (0.13 - 1)	8	0.18 (0.04 - 0.89)
Male	>12 to 16	19	0.60 (0.38 - 0.93)	30	0.41 (0.21 - 0.83)
Male	>16 to 20	51	0.77 (0.62 - 0.96)	36	0.64 (0.44 - 0.91)
Male	>20 to 24	15	0.87 (0.77 - 0.99)	2	0.79 (0.64 - 0.99)

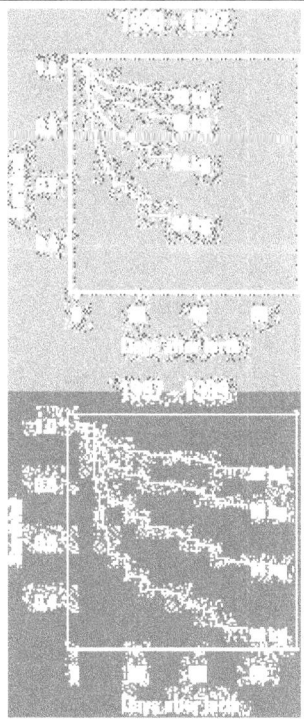

Figure 6. Elk calf survival by birth weight categories (sexes combined) during 1990 - 1992 and 1997 - 1999 (see Table 6 for sample sizes).

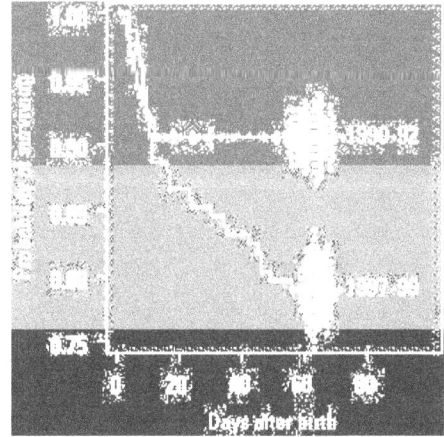

Figure 7. Estimated probability of an elk calf (sexes combined) of average birth weight (15.7 kg) not being killed by a predator during 1990 - 1992 and 1997 - 1999. Probability of death by predation is 1.0 minus the height of the curves. Tick marks indicate elk censored when transmitters were cast ($n = 19$ in 1990 - 1992 and $n = 1$ in 1997 - 1999) or calves surviving to 31 July of their birth year.

Table 7. Environmental and population characteristics of the two periods during which neonatal mortality of elk calves was studied in the Jackson herd.

Variable	Study period ($\bar{x} \pm$ SE) 1990 - 1992	1997 - 1999	Test result
Mean April temperature (°C)	5.1 ± 0.7	3.1 ± 0.2	$P = 0.05$
Mean number of days elk were fed on NER	66 ± 2.1	65.3 ± 9.1	$P = 0.95$
Mean daily ration fed to elk on NER (kg)	3.4 ± 0.3	3.3 ± 0.01	$P = 0.59$
Previous 5-year number of elk on and adjacent to National Elk Refuge in winter[a]	$8,681 \pm 567$	$10,558 \pm 360$	$P = 0.02$
Previous 5-year Jackson herd size[a]	$12,445 \pm 949$	$15,025 \pm 330$	$P = 0.03$

[a] Numbers of elk counted during mid-winter population surveys (Wyoming Game and Fish Department 2000), averaged for the five winters prior to the study period.

Table 8. Estimated annual recruitment rates (calves observed per 100 cows ≥ 1 year old) from two periods during which neonatal mortality of elk calves was studied in the Jackson herd. A hypothetical preparturition herd size of 11,000 elk (the state of Wyoming's herd management objective), pregnancy rate, and potential natality were held constant during the two study periods to evaluate the observed change in neonatal mortality on herd recruitment.

Variable	Study period ($\bar{x} \pm$ SE) 1990 - 1992	1997 - 1999	Test result
Herd pregnancy rate of females ≥1 year old[a]	63	63	
Potential natality	4,498	4,498	
% cohort mortality measured in radioed neonates	15.2	27.5	
Expected August recruitment[b]	53.4	45.7	
Observed August recruitment[c]	45.3 ± 1.7	34.7 ± 1.0	$P = 0.02$
Difference in observed and expected August recruitment	8.1	11.0	
% underestimation of mortality[d]	12.9	17.4	
Estimated neonatal mortalities[e]	1,264	2,020	
Observed mid-winter recruitment[f]	26.6 ± 1.7	20.6 ± 0.7	$P = 0.03$

[a] From Smith and Robbins (1994); pregnancy rate during 1998 - 2001 did not differ from the earlier period (see Results, Recruitment)

[b] Expected recruitment is the pregnancy rate reduced by the calculated neonatal mortality of radioed calves

[c] Observed recruitment is the number of calves:100 cows observed during August in the East and West study areas: 1990 - 1992 (Smith and Anderson 1996), 1997 - 1999 (BLS).

[d] This unaccounted for mortality largely is presumed to be perinatal mortality.

[e] Calf mortalities calculated as the difference between potential natality (63 calves:100 cows) in a herd of 11,000 elk and observed recruitment in August.

[f] Calves:100 cows observed in February on and adjacent to National Elk Refuge (Smith and McDonald 2002).

Recruitment

Pregnancy rate of elk ≥ 2 years old sampled during 1998 - 2002 (86.2% of 159 elk) did not differ ($X^2 = 0.03$, 1 df, $P = 0.8$) from 1978 - 1982 (87.1% of 318 elk). Likewise, pregnancy of yearlings was similar ($X^2 = 0.16$, 1 df, $P = 0.69$) during 1998 - 2002 (14.3% of 42 elk) and 1978 - 1982 (17.3% of 52 elk).

Summer and winter recruitment declined from the early 1990s to the late 1990s (Table 8). Early August calf:100 cow ratios in our study areas correlated with annual neonatal survival of radioed calves ($r^2 = 0.64$, $F_{1,4} = 7.06$, $P = 0.057$). Likewise, mid-winter calf:100 cow ratios (prior to when most winter

mortality occurs) of elk wintering on the NER correlated with neonatal survival ($r^2 = 0.62$, $F_{1,4} = 6.64$, $P = 0.062$). Calf:100 cow ratios during August in GTNP inversely correlated with population size (Figure 10). Calf:100 cow ratios on the NER during mid-winter also inversely correlated ($r^2 = 0.47$, $F_{1,15} = 13.1$, $P = 0.003$) with population size the previous winter (Figure 10). The inverse relationship between calf:100 cow ratios and the winter NER elk population strengthened ($r^2 = 0.58$, $F_{1,15} = 19.6$, $P = 0.001$) when a 2-year lag effect (t-2) was used to reflect the true recruitment from adult cows rather than adult cows plus yearling cows.

Rate of Increase and Harvestable Surplus

Increased neonatal mortality reduced the finite rate of increase of the elk population from May (beginning of parturition) to September (beginning of the elk hunting season) each year from 1.39 ± 0.004 during 1990 - 1992 to 1.34 ± 0.004 during 1997 - 1999 (mean ± 1 SD; Fisher's least significant difference, $P < 0.05$). Starting with a hypothetical preparturition herd size of 11,000 elk in May during both time periods, we simulated a September population of 15,274 ± 40 ($x ± 1$ SD) in the early 1990s compared to 14,786 ± 43 in the late 1990s. Therefore, the increased neonatal mortality observed during the late 1990s might lower the harvestable surplus by 486 elk if the population were at the state of Wyoming's management objective of 11,000 elk (Fisher's least significance difference, $P < 0.05$).

The annual finite rate of increase (λ) of the elk population declined slightly from 1.26 in the early 1990s to 1.23 in the late 1990s. The λ primarily was sensitive to adult female survival rate, and secondarily to calf survival rate in both the early and late 1990s (Table 9).

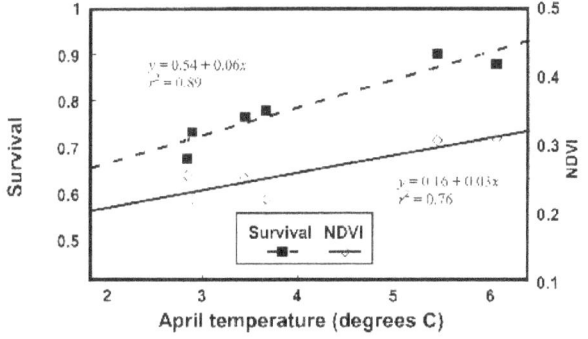

Figure 8. Relationship of mean monthly April temperature (^{0}C) to annual probability of survival from birth to 31 July of Jackson elk herd neonates, and to normalized difference vegetation index (NDVI) during the second and third weeks of April 1990 - 1992 and 1997 - 1999.

Table 9. Sensitivity analyses of Lefkovitch matrices of the Jackson elk herd, northwest Wyoming, constructed for the early 1990s and late 1990s. Here, $\frac{\partial \lambda}{\partial \alpha_{ij}}$ is the sensitivity of the finite rate of increase (λ) to changes in element a_{ij} of the Lefkovitch matrix. The larger the sensitivity index, $\frac{\partial \lambda}{\partial \alpha_{ij}}$, the more sensitive λ was to the vital rate.

Vital rate	1990 - 1992 $\frac{\partial \lambda}{\partial \alpha_{ij}}$	1997 - 1999 $\frac{\partial \lambda}{\partial \alpha_{ij}}$
Calf survival	0.34	0.36
Yearling female survival	0.23	0.22
Adult female survival	0.65	0.67
Yearling fecundity	0.09	0.08
Adult fecundity	0.26	0.24

A

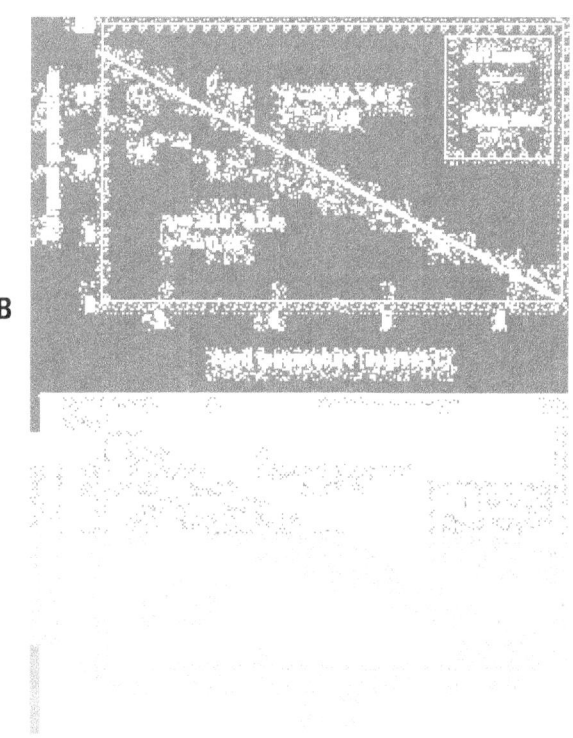

B

Figure 9. Predation by black bears and combined predation by black and grizzly bears on elk neonates of the Jackson herd, 1990 - 1992 and 1997 - 1999, related to mean monthly April temperature (A), and to normalized difference vegetation index (NDVI) during the second and third weeks of April (B).

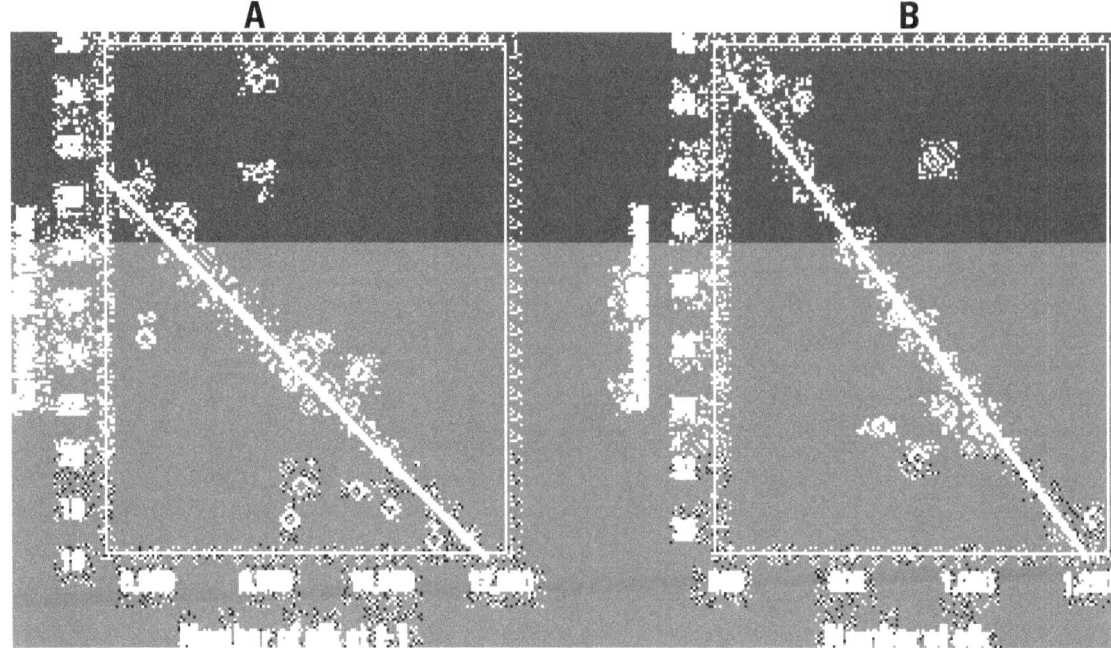

Figure 10. Calf:100 cow ratios at the National Elk Refuge during winters 1983 - 1999 regressed on number of elk counted on the National Elk Refuge the previous winter (A), and summer calf:100 cow ratios in Grand Teton National Park regressed on number of elk counted during summers 1991 - 1999 (B).

Elk calf in Wyoming. Bruce Smith/USFWS.

Discussion

Predisposing Mortality Factors

Birth weight strongly influenced survival of individual elk calves as in other studies of ungulates (Clutton-Brock et al. 1982, 1992, Clutton-Brock and Albon 1989, Kunkel and Mech 1994, Sams et al. 1996, Singer et al. 1997). Light-born calves were more vulnerable to all types of mortality, including predation. Male calves experienced higher mortality than females during the 6 years. As Smith and Anderson (1996) suggested, males may have been more rambunctious than females and consequently more subject to detection and mortality by predators than females during the early 1990s. Their faster growth rates and greater demand for milk may have prompted increased solicitations of nursing from their mothers, increasing exposure to predation. However, during the late 1990s, when growth rates were significantly reduced, predation was not sex-biased.

We unfortunately cannot compare blood chemistries between study periods, but we found several differences in serum values between calves that survived and calves that died during the late 1990s. Normal values and kinetics of serum enzymes and electrolytes from birth through weaning are not published for elk but have been examined for bovine calves (Knowles et al. 2000). Cross species comparisons must be made with care but the general pattern of increase and decline in ruminants is probably similar.

Physiological Status—Alkaline phosphatase is an enzyme widespread in the body in various isoforms. Our assays did not differentiate between isoenzymes derived from liver or bone. Serum alkaline phosphatase values are typically high in neonates compared to adults but considerable individual variation occurs. The mean values found in both groups of elk calves were within normal ranges determined for neonatal bovine calves suggesting that the values detected did not indicate disease (Knowles et al. 2000). Increased levels of alkaline phosphatase in the calves that survived may have been due to increased activity of osteoblasts and bone formation and thus reflect more active growth than the calves that did not survive.

Higher mean levels of serum glucose may indicate that calves that survived had more recently nursed and thus had better maternal care than the calves that did not survive. However, serum glucose is quite labile in whole blood samples and differences could reflect handling of the sample. Similarly,

lactate dehydrogenase values may be influenced by handling including hemolysis and freezing of samples (Kaneko 1989), although struggling and increased muscle activity during capture could also result in increased levels of lactate dehydrogenase.

Higher phosphorus levels in surviving calves may be related to skeletal mobilization and construction. Hemolysis may also influence levels of serum phosphorus.

Total protein typically decreases due to nutritional problems. Although surviving calves had higher total protein than those that died, the difference we measured in total protein between those groups was small.

Serum glutamyltransferase (GGT) is correlated with passive transfer of immunoglobulins in neonatal bovine calves. It is produced in the mammary gland and is present at high levels in colostrum and thus serum levels in neonates may serve as a marker for ingestion of colostrum. Higher levels of GGT were found in neonatal white-tailed deer (*Odocoileus virginianus*) that survived compared to fawns that died (Sams et al. 1996) and ingestion of colostrum was suggested as a factor improving survival. Colostrum contains immunoglobulins and ingestion thus provides neonates with passive immunity to pathogens in their environment. The levels of GGT found in our elk calves were similar to well-nourished white-tailed deer fawns but considerably lower than levels found in bovine neonates (Knowles et al. 2000), which may reflect species differences in mammary enzyme production. Levels of GGT did not differ between elk calves that survived and died.

Blood urea nitrogen (BUN) levels may be influenced by both levels of production and excretion. The BUN levels found in both groups of elk calves were within normal ranges, though calves that died had slightly higher levels of BUN than those that survived. Contrarily, surviving white-tailed deer fawns had higher levels of BUN than those killed by predators (Kunkel and Mech 1994). Levels of BUN in bovine calves are very dynamic during the first few weeks of life (Knowles et al. 2000). Protein catabolism from muscle may cause increased levels of BUN in undernourished animals and thus differences between groups of elk calves may reflect a decreased plane of nutrition in calves that did not survive.

In summary, differences we observed in serum chemistries between calves that survived and those that died may reflect better condition and/or higher intake of milk of surviving calves. This inference is consistent with nutritional studies at the Starkey Experimental Forest where lower levels of serum alkaline phosphatase, phosphorus, and glucose and elevated BUN correlated with poorer nutrition of elk neonates (J. G. Cook, pers. commun.).

Rate of Gain—Birth weights did not differ between the early and late 1990s, but calf growth rates and mortality did. The selective pressures of predation, hypothermia, and seasonal food restrictions have uniformly acted to produce relatively high neonatal milk intake; growth rates in temperate and arctic ungulates (Robbins and Robbins 1979). For example, Gerhart et al. (1996) reported that caribou calves attain their maximum genetic potential for daily weight gain during the first 4 weeks of life. Consequently, the highest energetic costs to female cervids occur during early lactation (Cowan and Wood 1955, Clutton-Brock and Albon 1989, Robbins and Robbins 1979, Spalinger 2000), and growth of calves is closely related to the milk yield of mothers (Mitchell et al. 1976, Blaxter and Hamilton 1980, Clutton-Brock and Albon 1989). Robbins et al. (1981) suggested that food intake of elk increases during late gestation and early lactation to compensate for decreased energy reserves following winter. Less than optimum foraging conditions and nutrition in several species of deer and domestic mammals will adversely affect the dam, her milk yield, and hence the growth rate, postnatal survival, and weaning weight of offspring (Clutton-Brock et al. 1982, Louden et al. 1983, Cameron et al. 1993, Cook et al. 2004).

Not only did mortality increase during the late 1990s (particularly among females), but calves remained vulnerable to mortality, particularly predation, for twice as long following birth (Figures 4, 6; Appendix B). Elk calves are hiders (Geist 1982). After they are big and strong enough to follow their mothers and join nursery groups, calves benefit from the protection afforded by adults from predators that employ search techniques similar to bears. Calves that grow slowly may be nutritionally compromised, remain dependent on the hider strategy longer, and be less capable of avoiding predation. Female calves, which had lower birth weights than males throughout the 1990s, may have suffered more than males from the reduced weight gains we measured during the late 1990s.

Weather—As in red deer (*Cervus elaphus*; Albon et al. 1987), our results suggest that neonatal survival was affected in a density-independent fashion by April temperatures -- not because of the influence of April temperatures on cohort birth weights but their influence on daily rates of gain immediately postpartum. We cannot unequivocally demonstrate the causative relationships between stochastic conditions, calf weight gains, and neonatal survival. We did not directly measure annual quality of forage available to elk during late gestation and early lactation, nor did we measure milk production of elk.

However, onset of forage green-up, as indicated by NDVI during April, was strongly related to April temperatures, and we hypothesize that post-winter recovery of body condition and milk production of mothers varied with spring green-up of vegetation. New vegetative growth generally first appears in Jackson Hole in April and is significantly more nutritious and digestible than cured forage and rations of alfalfa hay fed elk on NER (Smith et al. 1997). Merrill et al. (1993) reported that cool spring temperatures that delayed snowmelt retarded the onset of new plant growth by as much as one month in Yellowstone National Park. Cooler April temperatures during the late 1990s (a density-independent effect), possibly compounded by increased competition for high quality forage on winter ranges among larger numbers of elk (a density-dependent effect), may have been the ultimate factors responsible for diminished neonatal growth and survival in the Jackson elk herd.

Recruitment and Density Dependence

Adult survival of the Jackson elk herd is high, despite harvests averaging 3,050 elk annually during the 1990s (Smith and Anderson 1998, Wyoming Game and Fish Department 2000, Lubow and Smith 2004). Reduced survival of neonates, in combination with hunter harvest of antlerless elk, has produced a slow decline in the elk herd from 18,200 elk in 1997 toward the State of Wyoming's population objective of 11,029 elk (Lubow and Smith 2004).

Recruitment in ungulates is the main target of limiting factors, both density-dependent and density-independent (Gaillard et al. 1998). Houston (1982) and Singer et al. (1997) reported that both climate and population density influenced neonatal survival when the northern Yellowstone elk herd was near carrying capacity. Clutton-Brock et al. (1982) and Sæther (1997) concluded that density had a more significant influence on winter survival of calves than on neonatal survival. As numbers of red deer on Rhum increased, selection against light-born calves rose, despite no consistent change in cohort birth weights (Clutton-Brock et al. 1982). During the 1990s, we found calf:100 cow ratios during August in GTNP and mid-winter on the NER (where most elk from calving areas in which we worked spent winter, Smith 1994), were inversely related to population size, suggesting a density-dependent relationship in calf recruitment. Boyce (1989) reported similar findings prior to 1990. Rather than declining fecundity, which we found unchanged from the 1980s, the effect during our study was likely reduced juvenile survival. The August and mid-winter calf:100 cow ratios corroborated the trend, but not the amplitude, in annual neonatal survival (Table 8).

We modeled a decline between 1990 - 1992 and 1997 - 1999 of 486 calves (11%) from a potential recruitment of 4,498 elk resulting from the different rates of neonatal mortality we measured during those time periods. If we account for potentially unmeasured perinatal mortality by comparing expected and observed midsummer recruitment, estimated decline in recruitment was 756 elk (17%, Table 8). Gaillard et al. (1998) found that in 14 species of ungulates, juvenile survival varied more than adult survival. However, a change in adult survival had 3 times the effect on λ as an equivalent change in recruitment. Our findings suggest adult female survival had twice the effect on λ as a change in neonatal survival (Table 9).

We did not measure a functional response of either weight gain or mortality of neonates to increased herd size during our study. Increased competition for spring forage among adults or social stressors may have diminished milk yields; but retarded postnatal growth and increased mortality of calves may have resulted from other factors, such as reduced milk production due to delayed vegetative green-up, or more predators. Winter food supplementation of 70% of the Jackson elk herd confounds any influence of increased elk densities on calf survival (Lubow and Smith 2004). However, daily rations and duration of feeding of NER elk were no different between our two study periods, and presumably did not affect differentially the condition of adult female elk or subsequent growth rates of their offspring. Furthermore, Bailey (1999) compared elk that wintered off feedgrounds to elk fed on the NER during winters 1996-97 and 1997-98 and found no differences in pregnancy rates, fetal growth, or body condition of cow elk. Finally, population analyses by Lubow and Smith (2004) found strong support for weather-dependent neonatal survival but only weak evidence of density dependence in neonatal survival at the range of population sizes modeled in the Jackson elk herd from 1980 to 2002 (9,000 - 18,200).

As Sæther (1997) noted, density dependence is particularly difficult to detect and demonstrate in ungulates, which are long-lived and show a high degree of age dependence in fecundity and mortality. These age-specific effects may generate time lags of 3 - 10 years in density-dependent responses and increase the length of study required to detect responses. Due to the nonlinearity of density dependence (Fowler 1987), detection may require that populations approach or exceed carrying capacity, which the food-supplemented Jackson herd apparently did not during the 1990s (Lubow and Smith 2004).

Predation
In general, neonatal loses are high in ungulates and may result from high rates of predation (Linnell et al. 1995, Sæther 1997). We found 68% and 76% of mortality during 1990 - 1992 and 1997 - 1999, respectively, was due to predation. Black bears accounted for 11 of 15 predator kills and 50% of all mortality during 1990 - 1992, and at least 16 of 32 predator kills and 38% of all mortality during 1997 - 1999. Black bears, which can also be important predators of moose (Alces alces) (Ballard et al. 1981, Schwartz and Franzmann 1991) and white-tailed deer (Kunkel and Mech 1994, Ozoga and Clute 1988), accounted for 24 of 35 neonatal elk mortalities in Idaho (Schlegel 1976).

Singer et al. (1997) reported 75% of neonatal elk losses in Yellowstone National Park resulted from predation primarily by grizzly bears and coyotes. The 31% mortality of 127 radioed calves in Yellowstone is similar to the 27.5% loss we recorded during 1997 - 1999 when grizzly bears and mountain lions, in addition to black bears and coyotes, preyed on elk neonates. Gray wolves did not kill radioed neonates, but only one pack had colonized our study areas and not until the final year of our study.

Visitation rates at HCCs did not reflect relative predation rates on elk by black and grizzly bears. Black bears left 9 times more hair samples than grizzly bears at HCCs in the East SA, but killed 7 calves compared to 5 killed by grizzly bears (Table 6; Appendices A, C). Singer et al. (1997) noted that grizzly bears killed several times more elk neonates than did black bears in Yellowstone National Park where densities of the 2 bear species were roughly equivalent. Likewise, Ballard et al. (1988) and Larsen et al. (1989) found grizzly bears were more predatory than black bears on moose neonates in Alaska.

Bears are effective predators on neonatal ungulates and may either opportunistically develop this behavior or learn it from their mothers (Schlegel 1976, French and French 1990). Craighead and Sumner (1982) and French and French (1990) felt that grizzly bears may travel to elk calving areas in May and June specifically to prey on calves, presumably because the nutritional rewards are high. Alternatively, favorable phenological stage of plant communities may coincidentally draw elk and bears to similar areas to maximize nutrient intake from vegetation (Schlegel 1976).

Bear predation on elk increased during years with cooler April temperatures and lower April NDVI. Poor foraging conditions, due to delayed green-up may have prompted bears to find alternative food sources to meet nutritional requirements (Schwartz and Franzmann 1991). Reynolds and Garner (1987) hypothesized that caribou calves and carrion provided female bears a high protein food source when other foods were lower in nutrition and energy demands were high, especially for lactating females. French and French (1990) reported that sow grizzly bears with young preyed on elk calves more than their frequency in the population indicated, but Mattson (1997) reported male grizzly bears killed 2.8 elk calves/bear/year compared to 0.8 for female grizzly bears. Black bears appear to have higher growth, reproductive, and survival rates when neonatal ungulates are available as prey (Schwartz and Franzmann 1991). Thus in facultative predators, such as bears, predatory behavior may enhance fitness and therefore be adaptive. If so, predatory behavior should increase over time, as French and French (1990) suggested may have occurred among Yellowstone Park's grizzly bear population. However, Mattson's (1997) food habits analysis of Yellowstone grizzly bears did not support their contention.

In four published studies of neonatal elk mortality in our region, predator kills, primarily by bears, ceased by early July. Schlegel (1976) found 79% of predator losses, 94% of which were by black bears, occurred prior to 15 June when calves were < 21 days old. Singer et al. (1997) reported no calves > 28 days old were killed by grizzly or black bears. Of 60 grizzly bear predatory events on elk calves, French and French (1990) observed none after calves were > 34 days old. Mattson (1997) reported 71% of elk calf predation by grizzly bears in Yellowstone National Park occurred in June. We found the oldest calf killed during 1990 - 1992 by a predator, a black bear, was 12 days old. Calves 16 - 30 days of age died from causes other than predation. However, during the late 1990s, calves as much as 56 days old were killed by predators, including 5 predations by black and grizzly bears of calves 42 - 49 days old (Appendix B). We believe predators were able to successfully hunt older calves during the late 1990s due to increased vulnerability of those cohorts. Predation on calves of below average birth weight, lower growth rates, and inferior physiological condition suggests that predators found these calves vulnerable even when more than a month old.

We found that grizzly bears killed five of six calves before 19 June in advance of cattle turn-on dates in the Spread Creek allotment in Bridger-Teton National Forest and the Elk Ranch East allotment in GTNP. Depredations on bovine calves began in late June or July (Anderson et al. 2002), confirming some bears traveled to these allotments in advance of cattle being available. We do not know, however, if the same bears that killed elk were responsible for cattle depredations, nor do we know what proportion of the bear population preyed on either species. Moving cattle to adjacent, vacant grazing allotments on Bridger-Teton National Forest has been suggested to resolve grizzly bear depredations. We suggest this may only shift the location of the problem if the new allotment is used by calving elk. A better solution would be to move cattle beyond the known distribution of grizzly bears or to areas little used by elk for calving.

Reliability of Mortality Evaluation

Smith and Robbins (1994) estimated fecundity of elk that wintered on the NER at 63 calves:100 females $\geq$ 1 year old. Observed August calf:100 cow ratios of these elk, most of which calve in and adjacent to GTNP (Smith and Robbins 1994), averaged 45.3:100 during 1990 - 1992 compared to 53.4:100 expected following 15.2% neonatal mortality, and 34.7:100 during 1997 - 1999 compared to 45.7:100 expected following 27.5% mortality (Table 8).

Discrepancies between expected and observed recruitment are attributable to one or a combination of the following causes. 1) Measurement error or change in fecundity. Pregnancy rate of adult ($\geq$ 2 years old) females was nearly identical during 2 sampling periods (87.1%: 1978 - 1982; 86.5%: 1998 - 2001). The combined yearling and adult fecundity of 63 calves:100 females, corrected for *in*

utero and abortion losses, previously estimated for the Jackson herd (Smith and Robbins 1994) was statistically similar to the 60.4 calves: 100 females modeled by Lubow and Smith (2004) during the 1990s. Thus, unmeasured fecundity changes are an unlikely source of error. 2) Some barren cows may occupy habitats in midsummer in which they are less observable than calf-cow groups, thereby upwardly biasing observed recruitment estimates. Sightability corrected surveys of the Jackson elk herd conducted in 1996 did not indicate such a bias (Anderson et al. 1998). (3) Estimates of neonatal mortality of free-ranging ungulates from captured and radioed animals are downward-biased because of undetected perinatal mortality, including still births, calves rejected and abandoned by mothers, nonviable births, and perinatal predation. Ozoga and Clute (1988) concluded they underestimated by half all mortality of white-tailed deer from a sample of radio collared fawns. More than half of mortality of red deer and caribou (*Rangifer tarandus*) neonates occurs within 48 hours of birth (Blaxter and Hamilton 1980, Whitten et al. 1992).

Average age of our captured calves was 3.2 days and we surely missed the opportunity to capture some calves that died immediately postpartum. If we presume that recruitment discrepancies are largely due to this source, we underestimated mortality by an additional 13 - 17% of births (Table 8). Nonetheless, we detected several rarely reported causes of perinatal mortality, including dystocia, hemoperitoneum, enterocolitis due to *Coronavirus* and *Rotavirus*, brucellosis, encephalitis, meningitis, and a severe congenital cardiac anomaly (right ventricular aplasia; Appendices B, C). Two additional calves (388 and 399) sustained multiple abrasions associated with difficult births and were subsequently killed by a grizzly bear and coyote, respectively. These 14 calves ($\bar{x}$= 2.2 days old $\pm$ 0.3 SE) were younger (t = 3.1, P = 0.007) when captured than the remaining 284 calves ($\bar{x}$= 3.3 days old $\pm$ 0.1 SE), suggesting such rarely reported predisposing conditions are less likely to be found in neonates that have survived to an older age.

Compensation

Lower neonatal survival during the late 1990s was coincident with lower April mean monthly temperature, lower rates of gain of neonates, higher elk numbers, and ostensibly higher numbers of predators. We could not deduce the relative importance or interaction of these correlates with calf survival. Clearly, a greater proportion of calves died during the late 1990s, and the proximate cause of much of the mortality was predation. Population estimates of large carnivores are hard to come by, even in a region as intensively studied as Jackson Hole. The available information indicated numbers of grizzly bears (Anderson et al. 2002, Schwartz et al. 2002) and mountain lions (D. Brimeyer, and H. Quigley, pers. commun.) increased during our study. Nevertheless, black bears were responsible for most neonatal predation in both study areas and both study periods.

Grizzly bear and mountain lion predation during the late 1990s (4% and 1%, respectively, of radioed calves) could be considered additive mortality because predation rates by black bears and coyotes did not decline. However, five of six grizzly predations occurred in the East SA where total mortality was no greater than in our relatively grizzly bear-free West SA (Figure 3, Table 6). Importantly, diseases and accidents were four times less prevalent in the East SA than the West SA during the late 1990s (Figure 3). Suitable tissues for disease culture were seldom recoverable at bear kill sites, due to extensive feeding by bears. Yet, we diagnosed bacterial infections in calves 333 and 338 killed by a grizzly bear and black bear, respectively. Calf 388, killed by a grizzly bear, had experienced multiple abrasions during a difficult birth. This evidence suggests that some grizzly bear and other predation was compensatory, removing animals that were compromised and may have succumbed to other mortality. The extended temporal vulnerability of neonates during 1997 - 1999 supports such a conclusion, as does the lower birth weights among calves that died from predation (as well as victims

of disease and accidents) compared to calves that survived the neonatal period.

If grizzly bear predation and predation in general is partially compensatory, the net effect on the elk population may be much smaller than the absolute numbers of neonates killed by predation. That is, if predators remove compromised offspring that otherwise would succumb by fall to disease, accidents, or malnutrition, then the fall harvestable surplus may be little affected. Small calves are also disadvantaged in winter and suffer increased winter mortality (Clutton-Brock et al. 1982, Clutton-Brock and Albon 1989, Singer et al. 1997, Smith and Anderson 1998, Cook et al. 2004). However, exact compensation is rare and, further, compensation is influenced by population density (Sinclair and Pech 1996). Our findings suggest changes in recruitment and juvenile vulnerability to predation may ultimately be the products of stochastic variability in spring weather. Consequently, we can only conclude that increased predation was a proximate cause of declining neonatal survival during the 1990s.

A 3-day old elk with an expandable radio collar. Bruce Smith/USFWS.

Conclusion

Long-term predator-prey studies are essential to understanding the influence and interactions of variation in weather and population density on vulnerability of neonates to predation (Gaillard et al. 1998, Ballard et al. 2001). This is especially true in long-lived species, such as elk, with a high degree of age dependence in mortality and fecundity (Sæther 1997).

As in many multiple species systems, our findings do not clearly answer the question of how predators affect prey populations (Boutin 1992, Orians 1997), but suggest mechanisms by which some neonates are predisposed to predation and other mortality.

One explanation of our findings is that increased mortality of calves during the late 1990s occurred independently of their physiological condition and growth. More predators resulted in more mortality of calves. However, at high prey densities, predation may act in a depensatory fashion to limit but not regulate prey numbers (Sinclair and Pech 1996). Furthermore, kill rates of ungulate prey appear to depend on whether the predator species is an obligate or facultative carnivore. For obligate predators, such as wolves and mountain lions, per capita kill rates appear fairly consistent over a wide range of prey densities (Ballard et al. 2001). Only 2 of 64 mortalities during our study were by obligate predators. Kill rates of facultative carnivores, such

as bears and coyotes, may depend more on alternate food sources and prey density, particularly regarding predation on neonates (Schwartz and Franzmann 1991). For example, Mattson (1997) found annual use of ungulates as food by Yellowstone National Park grizzly bears was inversely related to availability and consumption of whitebark pine seed. Thus, the degree to which predation is compensatory is a product of predator numbers and relative abundance of alternate food sources.

We conclude that postpartum conditions for neonates declined during the 1990s resulting in birth of newborns that grew more slowly and suffered higher mortality during the two months postpartum. Slower growth extended the time during which calves were vulnerable to mortality, particularly predation. Low birth weight calves, particularly females, came under increasing and extended pressure of predation during the late 1990s. In short, adverse spring foraging conditions, for both predators and prey, possibly exacerbated by increased elk densities, may have precipitated a cascade of events that reduced calf recruitment. This scenario generates a complex model of predator-prey dynamics. The stochasitic ebb and flow of prey vulnerability and availability of alternate food sources for predators interact with predator abundance to dictate the degree to which predation is additive or compensatory over time.

Future Research

The continuing restoration and expansion of large carnivore populations in Jackson Hole, Wyoming, provide a unique opportunity to evaluate the interaction of a multi-predator community on a common prey species formerly released for several decades from predation by grizzly bears and gray wolves (Berger et al. 2001b). While predation on elk by black and grizzly bears and coyotes is largely restricted to neonates (Schlegel 1976, Singer et al. 1997), wolves and mountain lions are capable yearlong predators of juvenile and adult elk (Kunkel and Mech 1994, Murphy 1998, Kunkel et al. 1999, Smith et al. 1999). If predator numbers increase or the elk population declines, competition among these five extant carnivores, particularly during May - July, and pressure on recruitment will intensify, altering age structure of the elk herd. Given the economic importance of elk in this area (Smith 2001), a court-mandated environmental analysis of the elk winter feeding program (Urbina 1998), pending removal of grizzly bears and gray wolves from federal protection as threatened species, and keen public interest, we believe the following theses justify careful future evaluation.

a) Winter-spring predation by wolves and mountain lions could be partly compensatory with winter losses if predation is directed at nutritionally disadvantaged calves (Kunkel et al. 1999, Mech et al. 2001). If that predation focuses on elk not attending winter feedgrounds, and if wildlife managers respond by feeding additional elk to maintain population size, an increasing proportion of the elk herd will use feedgrounds in coming years. This has several ecological and economic consequences (Smith 2001).

b) Elk are a preferred prey of wolves and mountain lions in northern Rockies ecosystems (Kunkel et al. 1999, Murphy 1998, Mech et al. 2001). If elk numbers decline, alternate prey to elk will become more widely exploited by these predators (Kunkel and Pletscher 1999, Smith et al. 2000).

c) If predation on elk by a restored predator community in Jackson Hole is largely additive mortality, a decline in calf recruitment will require managers to make downward adjustments in human harvest of elk to maintain a stable population size (Gasaway et al. 1992, Kunkel and Pletscher 1999). However, if grizzly bears and wolves are delisted as threatened species, commensurate regulated harvest of these and the other predators of elk could maintain recruitment of elk.

d) Contrarily, if predation is largely compensatory, we will not see significant changes in the size of the elk population beyond those expected from human exploitation and variation in annual weather conditions, as modeled by Lubow and Smith (2004). As Sæther (1997) argued, more long-term investigations are needed to understand the complex interactions among ungulate recruitment, predation, weather, and nutrition. The Jackson herd provides one case study to compare with others in the northern Rocky Mountains.

Public interest in viewing large carnivores and commensurate economic benefits derived by states supporting carnivore populations have escalated during the past decade. Wildlife management decisions are now made under intense scrutiny by a public holding strong and divergent views on management (i.e. restoration, reintroduction, control) of large carnivores (Bath 1991, Fisher 1995, Orians 1997, U.S. Fish and Wildlife Service 1998). A skeptical public demands reliable information about how predators interact with ungulate populations, and insists on well-founded justifications for predator management programs. Meeting those needs are essential steps toward informed decision-making that balances public interests and maintains functional predator-prey systems.

Literature Cited

Albon, S. D., T. H. Clutton-Brock, and F. E. Guinness. 1987. Early development and population dynamics in red deer. II. Density-independent effects and cohort variation. Journal of Animal Ecology 56:69-81.

Anderson, C. R., D. S. Moody, B. L. Smith, F. G. Lindzey, and R. P. Lanka. 1998. Development and evaluation of sightability models for summer elk surveys. Journal of Wildlife Management 62:1055-1066.

Anderson, C. R., M. A. Ternent, and D. S. Moody. 2002. Grizzly bear-cattle interactions on two grazing allotments in northwest Wyoming. Ursus 13:247-256.

Bailey, J. R. 1999. A working model to assist in determining initiation of supplemental feeding of elk and a carrying capacity model for the National Elk Refuge, Jackson, Wyoming. M. S. Thesis, University of Wyoming, Laramie.

Ballard, W. B., T. H. Spraker, and K. P. Taylor. 1981. Causes of neonatal moose calf mortality in southcentral Alaska. Journal of Wildlife Management 45:335-342.

Ballard, W. B., S. D. Miller, and J. S. Whitman. 1988. Brown and black bear predation on moose in southcentral Alaska. Alces 26:1-8.

Ballard, W. B., D. Lutz, T. W. Keegan, L. H. Carpenter, and J. C. DeVos, Jr. 2001. Deer-predator relationships: a review of recent North American studies with emphasis on mule and black-tailed deer. Wildlife Society Bulletin 29:99-115.

Bangs, E. E. and S. H. Fritts. 1996. Reintroducing the gray wolf to central Idaho and Yellowstone National Park. Wildlife Society Bulletin 24:402-413.

Bartholow, J. 1997. POP-II system documentation, PC version 7. Fossil Creek Software, Fort Collins, Colorado.

Bath, A. J. 1991. Public attitudes in Wyoming, Montana, and Idaho toward wolf reintroduction in Yellowstone National Park. Pages 91-94 *in* Transactions of the Fifty-sixth North American Wildlife and Natural Resources Conference.

Berger, J., P. B. Stacey, L. Bellis, and M. P. Johnson. 2001a. A mammalian predator-prey imbalance: grizzly bear and wolf extinction affect avian neotropical migrants. Ecological Applications 11:947-960.

Berger, J., J. E. Swenson, and Inga-Lill Persson. 2001b. Recolonizing carnivores and naïve prey: conservation lessons from the Pleistocene extinctions. Science 291:1036–1039.

Blaxter, K. L., and W. J. Hamilton. 1980. Reproduction in farmed red deer. Calf growth and mortality. Journal of Agricultural Science 95:275-284.

Boutin, S. 1992. Predation and moose population dynamics: a critique. Journal of Wildlife Management 56:116-127.

Boyce, M. S. 1989. The Jackson herd: intensive wildlife management in North America. Cambridge University Press, Cambridge, U.K.

Braun, C. L. 1991. Mountain lion-human interaction symposium. Colorado Division of Wildlife, Denver, Colorado.

Cameron, R. D., W. T. Smith, S. G. Fancy, K. L. Gerhart, and R. G. White. 1993. Calving success of female caribou in relation to body weight. Canadian Journal of Zoology 71:480- 486.

Caswell, H. 2001. Matrix Population Models. 2nd edition. Sinauer Associates, Sunderland, Massachusetts.

Caughley, G. 1977. Analysis of vertebrate populations. John Wiley and Sons, New York, New York.

Clark, T., P. C. Griffin, and S. Minta. 1999. Carnivores in ecosystems: the Yellowstone experience. Yale University, New Haven, Connecticut.

Clutton-Brock, T. H., F. E. Guinness, and S. D. Albon. 1982. Red deer: behavior and ecology of two sexes. University of Chicago Press, Chicago, Illinois.

Clutton-Brock, T. H., and S. D. Albon. 1989. Red deer in the Highlands. Blackwell Scientific Publications, Oxford, U.K.

Clutton-Brock, T. H., O. F. Price, S. D. Albon, and P. A. Jewell. 1992. Early development and population fluctuations in Soay sheep. Journal of Animal Ecology 61:381-396.

Cole, G. F. 1969. The elk of Grand Teton and southern Yellowstone National Parks. National Park Service, Research Report GRTE-N-1, Washington, DC.

Collett, D. 1994. Modeling survival data in medical research. Chapman and Hall, London, U.K.

Cook, J. G., B. K. Johnson, R. C. Cook, R. A. Riggs, T. Delcurto, L. D. Bryant, and L. L. Irwin. 2004. Effects of summer-autumn nutrition and parturition date on reproduction and survival of elk. Wildlife Monographs 155:1-61.

Cox, D. R. and Oakes, D. 1984. Analysis of survival data. Chapman and Hall, London, U.K.

Cowan, I. McT., and A. J. Wood. 1955. The growth rate of black-tailed deer. Journal of Wildlife Management 19:331-336.

Craighead, J. J., and J. S. Sumner. 1982. Evaluation of grizzly bear food plants, food categories, and habitat. Pages 44–84 in J. J. Craighead, J. S. Sumner, and G. B. Scaggs, editors. A definitive system for analysis of grizzly bear habitat and other wilderness resources utilizing Landsat multispectral imagery and computer technology. Wildlife–Wildlands Institute Monograph 1. University of Montana, Missoula.

Estes, J. A. 1996. Predators and ecosystem management. Wildlife Society Bulletin 24:390-396.

Fisher, H. 1995. Wolf wars. Falcon Press, Helena and Billings, Montana.

Fowler, C. W. 1987. A review of density-dependence in populations of large mammals. Pages 401–441 in H. H. Genoways, editor. Current Mammalogy. Plenum, New York, New York.

French, S. P., and M. G. French. 1990. Predatory behavior of grizzly bears feeding on elk calves in Yellowstone National Park. International Conference on Bear Research and Management 8:335-341.

Gaillard, J. M., M. Festa-Bianchet, and N. G. Yoccoz. 1998. Population dynamics of large herbivores: variable recruitment with constant adult survival. Trends in Ecology and Evolution 13:58-63.

Garrott, R. A., R. M. Bartmann, and G. C. White. 1985. Comparison of radio-transmitter packages relative to deer fawn mortality. Journal of Wildlife Management 49:758-759.

Gasaway, W. C., R. D. Boertje, D. V. Grangaard, D. G. Kellyhouse, R. O. Stephenson, and D. F. Larsen. 1992. The role of predation in limiting moose at low densities in Alaska and Yukon and implications for conservation. Wildlife Monograph 120:1-59.

Geist, V. 1971. Mountain sheep: a study in behavior and evolution. University of Chicago Press, Chicago, Illinois.

Geist, V. 1982. Adaptive behavioral strategies. Pages 219-278 in J.W. Thomas and D.E. Toweill, editors. North American elk: ecology and management. Stackpole Books, Harrisburg, Pennsylvania.

Gerhart, K. L., R. G. White, R. D. Cameron, and D. E. Russell. 1996. Body composition and nutrient reserves of arctic caribou. Canadian Journal of Zoology 74:136-146.

Grambsch, P. and T. Therneau, 1994. Proportional hazards tests and diagnostics based on weighted residuals. Biometrika 81:515-26.

Holm, G. W. 1998. Interactions of sympatric black and grizzly bears in northwest Wyoming. M. S. Thesis, University of Wyoming, Laramie.

Houston, D. B. 1982. The Northern Yellowstone Elk. Macmillan Publishing, New York, New York.

Johnson, D. E. 1951. Biology of the elk calf, *Cervus canadensis*. Journal of Wildlife Management 15:396-410.

Kaneko, J. J. 1989. Clinical biochemistry of domestic animals, 4th edition. Academic Press, New York, New York.

Knowles, T. G., J. E. Edwards, K. J. Bazeley, S. N. Brown, A. Butterworth, and P. D. Wariss. 2000. Changes in the blood biochemical and haematological profile of neonatal calves with age. The Veterinary Record 147:593-598.

Kunkel, K. E., and L. D. Mech. 1994. Wolf and bear predation on white-tailed deer fawns in northeastern Minnesota. Canadian Journal of Zoology 72:1557-1565.

Kunkel, K. E., T. K. Ruth, D. H. Pletscher, and M. G. Hornocker. 1999. Winter prey selection by wolves and cougars in and near Glacier National Park, Montana. Journal of Wildlife Management 63:901-910.

Kunkel, K. and D. H. Pletscher. 1999. Species-specific population dynamics of cervids in a multi-predator ecosystem. Journal of Wildlife Management 63:1082-1093.

Larsen, D. G., and D. A. Gauthier. 1989. Effects of capturing pregnant moose and calves on calf survivorship. Journal of Wildlife Management 53:564-567.

Larsen, D. G., D. A. Gauthier, and R. L. Markel. 1989. Causes and rate of moose mortality in the Southwest Yukon. Journal of Wildlife Management 53:548-557.

Lefkovitch, L.P. 1965. The study of population growth in organisms grouped by stages. Biometrics 21:1-18.

Linnell, J. D. C., R. Aanes, and R. Andersen. 1995. Who killed Bambi? The role of predation in the neonatal mortality of temperate ungulates. Wildlife Biology 1:209- 223.

Louden, A. S. I., A. S. McNeilly, and J. A. Milne. 1983. Nutrition and lactational control in red deer. Nature 302:45-147.

Lubow, B. C., and B. L. Smith. 2004. Population dynamics of the Jackson elk herd. Journal of Wildlife Management 68:810-827.

Malingreau, J. P., and A. S. Belward. 1992. Scale considerations in vegetation monitoring using AVHRR data. International Journal of Remote Sensing 13:2289-2307.

Mattson, D. J. 1997. Use of ungulates by Yellowstone grizzly bears. Biological Conservation 81:161-177.

McNaughton, S. J. 1985. Ecology of a grazing ecosystem: the Serengeti. Ecological Monographs 55:259-294.

Mech, L. D. 1996. A new era for carnivore conservation. Wildlife Society Bulletin 24:397-401.

Mech, L. D., D. W. Smith, K. M. Murphy, and D. R. MacNulty. 2001. Winter severity and wolf predation on a formerly wolf-free elk herd. Journal of Wildlife Management 65:998-1003.

Merrill, E. H., M. K. Bramble-Brodahl, R. W. Marrs, and M. S. Boyce. 1993. Estimation of green herbaceous phytomass from Landsat MSS data in Yellowstone National Park. Journal of Range Management 46:151-157.

Mills, L. S., K. L. Pilgrim, and M. K. Schwartz, and K. McKelvey. 2000. Identifying lynx and other North American felids based on mtDNA analysis. Conservation Genetics 1:285-288.

Mitchell, B., D. McCowan, and I. A. Nicholson. 1976. Annual cycles of body weight and condition in Scottish red deer. Journal of Zoology 180:107-127.

Moore, T. D., L. E. Spence, and C. E. Dougnolle. 1974. Identification of dorsal guard hairs of some mammals of Wyoming. Wyoming Game and Fish Department Bulletin 14. Laramie, Wyoming.

Murphy, K. M. 1998. The ecology of the cougar (*Puma concolor*) in the northern Yellowstone Ecosystem: interactions with prey, bears, and humans. Ph.D. dissertation, University of Idaho, Moscow.

National Oceanic and Atmospheric Administration. 1992. Monthly station normals of temperature, precipitation, and heating and cooling degree-days, Wyoming, 1961 – 1990. National Climatic Data Center, Asheville, North Carolina. <http://www5.ncdc.noaa.gov> (10 January 2006).

Noyes, J. H., R. G. Sasser, B. K. Johnson, L. D. Bryant, and B. Alexander. 1997. Accuracy of pregnancy detection by serum protein (PSPB) in elk. Wildlife Society Bulletin 25:695-698.

Oldemeyer, J. L., R. L. Robbins, and B. L. Smith. 1993. Effect of feeding level on elk weights and reproductive success at the National Elk Refuge. Pages 64–68 *in* R. Callas, D. Koch, and E. Loft, editors. Western states and provinces elk workshop. California Fish and Game Department, Eureka, California.

Orians, G. H. 1997. Wolves, bears, and their prey in Alaska. National Academy Press, Washington, DC.

Ozoga, J.J., and R. K Clute, 1988. Mortality rates of marked and unmarked fawns. Journal of Wildlife Management 52:549-551.

Pate, J., M. J. Manfredo, A. D. Bright, and F. Tischbein. 1996. Coloradans' attitudes toward reintroducing the gray wolf into Colorado. Wildlife Society Bulletin 24:421-428.

Pettorelli, N., R. B. Weladji, O. Holand, A. Mysterud, J. Breie, and N. C. Stenseth. 2005. The relative role of winter and spring conditions: linking climate and landscape-scale plant phenology to alpine reindeer body mass. Biology Letters 1:24-26.

Power, M. E., D. Tilman, J. A. Estes, B. A. Menge, W. J. Bond, L. S. Mills, G. Daily, J. C. Castilla, J. Lubchenco, and R. T. Paine. 1996. Challenges in the quest for keystones. Bioscience 46:609-620.

Ralls, K., K. Brugger, and J. Ballou. 1979. Inbreeding and juvenile mortality in small populations of ungulates. Science 206:1101-1103.

Reed, B. C., J. F. Brown, D. VanderZee, T. R. Loveland, J. W. Merchant, and D. O. Ohlen. 1994. Measuring phenological variability from satellite imagery. Journal of Vegetation Science 5:703-714.

Reynolds, H. V., and G. W. Garner. 1987. Patterns of grizzly bear predation on caribou in northern Alaska. International Conference on Bear Research and Management 7:59-67.

Robbins, C. T., and B. L. Robbins. 1979. Fetal and neonatal growth patterns and maternal reproductive effort in ungulates and subungulates. American Naturalist 114:101-116.

Robbins, C. T, R. S. Podbielancik-Norman, D. L. Wilson, and E. D. Mould. 1981. Growth and nutrient consumption of elk calves compared to other ungulate species. Journal of Wildlife Management 45:172-186.

Sæther, B-E. 1997. Environmental stochasticity and population dynamics of large herbivores: a search for mechanisms. Trends in Ecology and Evolution 12:143-149.

Sams, M. G., R. L. Lochmiller, C. W. Qualls, Jr., D. M. Leslie, and M. E. Payton. 1996. Physiological correlates of neonatal mortality in an overpopulated herd of white-tailed deer. Journal of Mammalogy 77:179-190.

Schlegel, M. 1976. Factors affecting calf elk survival in northcentral Idaho — a progress report. Western Association of State Game and Fish Commissioners 56:342-355.

Schwartz, C. S., and A. W. Franzmann. 1991. Interrelationship of black bears to moose and forest succession in the northern coniferous forest. Wildlife Monograph 113:1-58.

Schwartz, C. S., and M. A. Haroldson. 2002. Yellowstone grizzly bear investigations. 2001 report of the Interagency Grizzly Bear Study Team. U.S. Department of Interior, U.S. Geological Survey, Bozeman, Montana.

Schwartz, C. S., M. A. Haroldson, K. Gunther, and D. S. Moody. 2002. Distribution of grizzly bears in the Greater Yellowstone Ecosystem, 1990-2000. Ursus 13:203-212.

Sinclair, A. R. E., and M. Norton-Griffiths. 1979. Serengeti: dynamics of an ecosystem. University Chicago Press, Chicago, Illinois.

Sinclair, A. R. E., and R. P. Pech. 1996. Density dependence, stochasticity, and predator regulation. Oikos 75:16-173.

Singer, F. J., A. T. Harting, and K. K. Symonds. 1997. Density-dependence, compensation, and environmental effects on elk calf mortality in Yellowstone National Park: Journal of Wildlife Management 61:12-25.

Smith, B. L. 1994. Population regulation of the Jackson elk herd. Ph.D. dissertation, University of Wyoming, Laramie.

Smith, B. L. 2001. Winter feeding of elk in western North America. Journal of Wildlife Management 65:173-190.

Smith, B. L. and S. H. Anderson. 1996. Patterns of neonatal mortality of elk in northwestern Wyoming. Canadian Journal of Zoology 74:1229-1237.

Smith, B. L. and S. H. Anderson. 1998. Juvenile survival and population regulation of the Jackson elk herd. Journal of Wildlife Management 62:1036-1045.

Smith, B. L. and S. H. Anderson. 2001. Does dispersal help regulate the Jackson elk herd? Wildlife Society Bulletin 29:331-341.

Smith, B. L., W. P. Burger, and F. J. Singer. 1998. An expandable radio collar for elk calves. Wildlife Society Bulletin 26:113-117.

Smith, B. L., and T. L. McDonald. 2002. Criteria for improving field classification of antlerless elk. Wildlife Society Bulletin 30:200-207.

Smith, B. L., and R. L. Robbins. 1994. Migrations and management of the Jackson elk herd. National Biological Survey Resource Publication 199, Washington, D.C.

Smith, B. L, R. L. Robbins, and S. H. Anderson. 1996. Adaptive sex ratios: another example? Journal of Mammalogy 77:818-825.

Smith, B. L, R. L. Robbins, and S. H. Anderson. 1997. Early development of supplementally fed, free-ranging elk. Journal of Wildlife Management 61:27-39.

Smith, D. W., K. M. Murphy, and D. S. Guernsey. 1999. Yellowstone Wolf Project: Annual Report, 1998, YCR-NR-99-1. National Park Service, Yellowstone Center for Resources, Yellowstone National Park, Wyoming.

Smith, D. W., L. D. Mech, M. Meagher, W. E. Clark, R. Jaffe, M. K. Phillips, and J. A. Mack. 2000. Wolf-bison interactions in Yellowstone National Park. Journal of Mammalogy 81:1128-1135.

Souvigney, J-M., K. Lackey, and S. C. Torbit. 1997. Concerns about wildlife and brucellosis in the Greater Yellowstone Area: a conservation perspective. Pages 161–168 *in* E. T. Thorne, M. S. Boyce, P. Nicoletti, and T. J. Kreeger, editors. Brucellosis, bison, elk, and cattle in the Greater Yellowstone Area: defining the problem, exploring solutions. Pioneer Printing, Cheyenne, Wyoming.

Spalinger, D. E. 2000. Nutritional Ecology. Pages 108-139 *in* S. Demarais, and P. R. Krausman, editors. Ecology and management of large mammals in North America. Prentice Hall, Upper Saddle River, New Jersey.

Toman, T. L., T. Lemke, L. Kuck, B. L. Smith, S. G. Smith, and K. Aune. 1997. Elk in the Greater Yellowstone Area: status and management. Pages 56–64 *in* E. T. Thorne, M. S. Boyce, P. Nicoletti, and T. J. Kreeger, editors. Brucellosis, bison, elk, and cattle in the Greater Yellowstone Area: defining the problem, exploring solutions. Pioneer Printing, Cheyenne, Wyoming.

Urbina, R. M. 1998. The Fund for Animals versus Jamie Rappaport Clark et al. Case number 98cv2355. United States District Court for the District of Columbia, Washington, DC.

U.S. Fish and Wildlife Service. 1998. Summary of public comments on the draft environmental impact statement for grizzly bear recovery in the Bitterroot Ecosystem. U.S. Fish and Wildlife Service, Missoula, Montana.

U.S. Fish and Wildlife Service. 2003. Final conservation strategy for the grizzly bear in the Yellowstone ecosystem. U.S. Fish and Wildlife Service, Missoula, Montana.

Weaver, J. L. 1977. Coyote-food base relationships in Jackson Hole, Wyoming. M.S. Thesis, Utah State University, Logan.

Whitten, K.R., G. W. Garner, F. J. Mauer, and R. B. Harris. 1992. Productivity and early calf survival in the Porcupine caribou herd. Journal of Wildlife Management 56:201-212.

Woods, J. G., D. Paetkau, D. Lewis, B. N. McLellan, M. Proctor, and C. Strobeck. 1999. Genetic tagging of free-ranging black and brown bears. Wildlife Society Bulletin 27:616-627.

Wyoming Game and Fish Department. 1996. Effectiveness of attractants to lure grizzly bears into hair collection sites for future DNA fingerprinting—the Blackrock/Spread Creek area study. Wyoming Game and Fish Department, Lander, Wyoming.

Wyoming Game and Fish Department. 2000. Annual big game herd unit reports, Region 1. Wyoming Game and Fish Department, Cheyenne, Wyoming.

Appendix A.

Frequency of visitation (proportion of weeks visited during the sampling period) of black and grizzly bears at hair collection corrals in the East and West study areas during 1997 - 1999. We monitored all corrals weekly from approximately 1 June through 31 July 1998 and 1999 (8 weeks). In 1997, we monitored all hair collection corrals 1 June through the third week of July (7 weeks) except Granite Creek and Death Canyon, which we monitored only during July (4 weeks).

Corral Name	Study Area	Species	Frequency of visitation[a]		
			1997	1998	1999
Murie Ridge	West	Black bear	0.71	0.75	0.88
Timbered Island	West	Black bear	0	0.13	0.63
Timbered Island	West	Grizzly bear	0	0	0.13
Burned Ridge	West	Black bear	0.29	0.50	0
RKO Road	West	Black bear	0.57	0.13	0
River Road	West	Black bear	0.29	0.13	0.38
River Road	West	Grizzly bear	0	0.13	0
Death Canyon	West	Black bear	1.00	0	0.13
Death Canyon	West	Grizzly bear	0	0	0.13
Granite Creek	West	Black bear	0.50	0.25	0.50
Three Rivers	East	Black bear	0	0.25	0.25
Three Rivers	East	Grizzly bear	0	0	0.13
Wolf Ridge	East	Black bear	0	0	0.25
Lava Creek	East	Black bear	0.57	0.63	0.13
Wallace Draw	East	Black bear	0	0	0.38
Mary's Lake	East	Black bear	0.14	0	0.13
Mary's Lake	East	Grizzly bear	0	0.13	0
All corrals	West	Black bear	0.48	0.27	0.36
All corrals	East	Black bear	0.14	0.18	0.23
All corrals	West	Grizzly bear	0	0.02	0.04
All corrals	East	Grizzly bear	0	0.03	0.03

[a] Number of weeks when hair was collected divided by the total number of weeks that we monitored hair corrals

Appendix B.

Cause-specific mortality of radioed neonatal elk from the Jackson elk herd, northwest Wyoming, that died during 1990 - 1992 (n = 22 of 145 calves) and 1997 - 1999 (n = 42 of 153 calves).

Mortality class	Specific cause	Number (%) of elk that died			
		1990 - 1992		1997 - 1999	
Predation	Black bear	11	(50)	16	(38)
	Coyote	4	(18)	5	(12)
	Grizzly bear			6	(14)
	Lion			2	(5)
	Unknown predator			2	(5)
	Unknown bear			1	(2)
	Subtotal	15	(68)	32	(76)
Accidents	Drowned	1		2	
	Dystocia			1	
	Hemoperitoneum			1	
	Subtotal	1	(5)	4	(10)
Disease	Bacterial pneumonia	1		3	
	Viral enterocolitis	3			
	Meningitis			1	
	Brucellosis-encephalitis			1	
	Congenital heart defect[a]			1	
	Emaciation	1			
	Starvation	1			
	Subtotal	6	(27)	6	(14)
Grand total		22	(100)	42	(100)

[a] Calf born without a right ventricle.

Appendix C.

Causes of and age at death of 22 of 145 elk neonates (sorted by dates of death) that died during 1990 - 1992 and 42 of 153 neonates that died during 1997 - 1999 in the East (E) and West (W) study areas.

Year	Sex	Study area	Calf no.	Cause of death	Date	Days old
1990	F	W	20	Black bear	5 June	12
1990	M	E	42	Coyote	8 June	8
1990	M	E	47	Black bear	13 June	7
1990	F	E	44	Starvation	4 July	30
1990	F	W	53	Bacterial pneumonia	15 July	20
1991	F	W	55	Black bear	29 May	10
1991	M	E	67	Black bear	31 May	4
1991	M	W	71	Black bear	1 June	5
1991	M	W	70	Black bear	2 June	4
1991	M	W	82	Black bear	3 June	6
1991	M	E	58	Black bear	5 June	12
1991	M	W	69	Black bear	7 June	9
1991	F	W	90	Coyote	7 June	6
1991	M	W	104	Emaciation	9 June	4
1991	M	E	97	Enterocolitis - coronavirus	20 June	16
1991	F	W	74	Black bear	21 June	3
1991	M	W	101	Enterocolitis - coronavirus	23 June	18
1992	M	E	121	Coyote	30 May	3
1992	M	W	131	Coyote	1 June	2
1992	M	E	134	Black bear	2 June	5
1992	M	W	130	Drowned	22 June	24
1992	M	E	160	Enterocolitis - rotavirus	28 June	24
1997	F	W	346	Brucellosis-encephalitis	31 May	1
1997	M	E	320	Unknown predator	3 June	8
1997	M	E	334	Dystocia	4 June	3
1997	F	E	333	Grizzly bear	6 June	9
1997	M	W	341	Coyote	8 June	4
1997	F	W	325	Black bear	10 June	11
1997	M	E	317	Black bear	15 June	16
1997	M	W	339	Bacterial broncho-pneumonia	18 June	14

Year	Sex	Study area	Calf no.	Cause of death	Date	Days old
1997	F	E	301	Grizzly bear	18 June	23
1997	M	W	342	Drowned	23 June	24
1997	M	E	335	Black bear	24 June	24
1997	M	W	324	Mountain lion	7 July	35
1997	F	W	329	Meningitis	7 July	37
1997	M	W	303	Black bear	9 July	45
1997	F	W	338	Black bear	17 July	46
1998	F	W	368	Hemoperitoneum	31 May	6
1998	F	W	367	Congestive heart failure[a]	2 June	6
1998	F	E	369	Unknown bear	2 June	6
1998	F	E	374	Grizzly bear	3 June	8
1998	F	E	394	Black bear	8 June	6
1998	M	E	397	Black bear	10 June	8
1998	M	W	379	Mountain lion	10 June	10
1998	M	E	387	Black bear	11 June	9
1998	M	E	347	Black bear	11 June	17
1998	F	W	377	Black bear	12 June	11
1998	F	E	388	Grizzly bear	19 July	49
1998	M	W	383	Unknown predator	22 July	56
1999	F	W	416	Black bear	28 May	3
1999	M	W	400	Coyote	29 May	4
1999	M	W	415	Coyote	31 May	7
1999	M	E	420	Black bear	7 June	9
1999	F	E	425	Grizzly bear	7 June	11
1999	M	W	450	Black bear	9 June	7
1999	F	W	432	Grizzly bear	14 June	17
1999	M	E	452	Coyote	16 June	10
1999	M	E	453	Bacterial broncho-pneumonia	24 June	17
1999	M	W	399	Coyote	26 June	34
1999	F	W	401	Black bear	30 June	30
1999	M	W	436	Drowned	12 July	45
1999	F	W	445	Bacterial broncho-pneumonia	13 July	40
1999	F	W	438	Black bear	14 July	42
1999	F	W	437	Black bear	16 July	46

[a] Calf born without a right ventricle.

U.S. Department of the Interior
U.S. Fish & Wildlife Service

http://www.fws.gov

September 2006